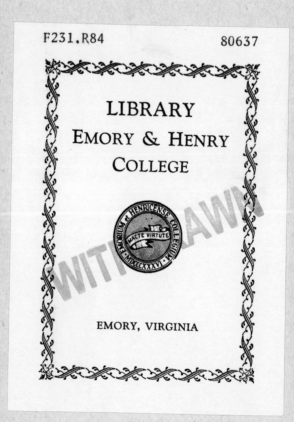

NEW ROADS IN OLD VIRGINIA

ROCKBRIDGE COUNTY

NEW ROADS IN OLD VIRGINIA

BY
AGNES ROTHERY

WITH ILLUSTRATIONS BY
ALICE ACHESON

BOSTON AND NEW YORK
HOUGHTON MIFFLIN COMPANY
The Riverside Press Cambridge
1929

The Riverside Press
CAMBRIDGE · MASSACHUSETTS
PRINTED IN THE U.S.A.

TO

SIDNEY

WHO LOVES VIRGINIA

FOREWORD

IT is difficult for most Americans, well-grounded in the story of the Boston Tea Party, and familiar from childhood with every breathless syllable of Paul Revere's ride, to realize that New England was not the only stage for the struggle for independence. It is difficult for visitors from the Middle West and the Coast, finding markers and monuments on every historic spot throughout Massachusetts, New Jersey, and Pennsylvania, to appreciate Virginia's rôle in the building of our Republic. They know that she furnished four out of our first five Presidents and that Cornwallis surrendered at Yorktown, but as for the integral spirit of the State, they are comfortably ignorant. For the Virginians have never been self-advertisers. It has been enough for them to have been conscious of their richly overlaid traditions and to enjoy the sunny happiness of their present. Although they are personally hospitable, they are not eager to exploit their State — its beauty or its history — to a touring public. Privacy and leisure have always seemed more desirable to them than the money

such exploitation might bring to the general
treasury.

But the automobile is no respecter of either
privacy or leisure. There are good roads through
Virginia now, and on each of them is threaded a
succession of superb views and historical anecdote.
And mountains and valleys alike, in every season of
the year, are enveloped in a climate of such soft and
gentle brightness that it steals into the senses of
even the most casual traveler, and is never quite
forgotten. It is for these transients, forced into
haste by the pressure of modern life, and forgetting
in the stress of maturity certain schoolday chapters
of the past, that this book is written.

CONTENTS

PART I
A GLIMPSE OF TIDEWATER VIRGINIA

PART II
THROUGH PIEDMONT VIRGINIA

PART III
UP THE SHENANDOAH VALLEY

ILLUSTRATIONS

NEW ROADS IN OLD VIRGINIA

. .
.

PART I
A GLIMPSE OF TIDEWATER VIRGINIA

NEW ROADS IN OLD VIRGINIA

.·.

CHAPTER I

ALEXANDRIA, THE COLONIAL CITY

ALEXANDRIA is the logical geographical point from which to enter Virginia — whether the trip is to be along the Tidewater country, or through the Piedmont region, or up the Shenandoah Valley. It is the logical point historically speaking as well, for it was a trim and flourishing town when Washington was still an unmapped marsh and possessed a consequential port whose business was frequently compared to that of New York — to the disadvantage of the latter. And for the antiquarian it is one of the treasure spots of America, with old-fashioned streets lined by pre-Revolutionary buildings; white clapboarded houses whose H-hinged front doors looked out disapprovingly on the red-coated British; fine mansions over whose polished floors stepped officers of the new little American army and Presidents of the new little American Republic; and rows of circumspect city houses, built closely together with exquisitely carved porticoes and finely wrought iron grilles.

At first glance Alexandria seems almost like a toy village, so bravely do the worn brass knockers shine, so trimly cut are the century-old box hedges. One still sees cobbled alleys with open gutters down the center, and in spite of automobiles and new hotels the general impression is one of two-story buildings, put together with the staunchness and finish that were the early craftsman's pride. There is a grateful absence of that architecture prevalent at what has been succinctly summarized as 'the spittoon period' of American culture. Mansions, cottages, city houses, and public buildings have

ALEXANDRIA, WITH OLD-FASHIONED STREETS LINED BY PRE-REVOLUTIONARY BUILDINGS

somehow been preserved in such entirety and numbers as still to stamp the city as Colonial. The names of the streets intensify the illusion, for they were given when the inhabitants still loved royalty: King, Prince, Duke, Queen, Royal, and Princess. Cameron was for Lord Fairfax, Baron of Cameron. A little later they were to name their new thoroughfares for Washington, Jefferson, Madison, and Lee. Wilkes, a member of Parliament who had suffered in defense of the Colonies, is perpetuated in syllables spoken a thousand times a day: so is Pitt, the Premier who loved liberty, and the Bishop of St. Asaph, who wrote in favor of Colonial independence. Thus a consecutive story of early American history is hourly sustained by the speech of Alexandria.

This adorable city, neatly patterned along the banks of the Potomac, is peculiarly Washington's home town. It was here that he maintained the town house so frequently mentioned in his diary, owned and rented tenements, served as vestryman and on the city board of trustees, and became a member of the Masonic Lodge. His interest expressed itself in various practical ways. He organized the Friendship Fire Company and presented it with the best engine procurable. He insisted upon the use of standard weights and measures in the market, and chose his closest friends and his lifelong physician from Alexandria men. He attended the Birthnight Balls in honor of the King and Queen at Gadsby's Tavern, and had his headquarters and received his first command in the building still to be seen on Royal Street.

Concrete as was his affiliation with the town, which at that time acknowledged only Boston as a rival, it might have passed into mere verbal tradition had not so many actual mementoes been preserved. Washington's personality, as it is transmitted to us of the present day through his calm portraits, his formal statues, and his measured utterances, lacks the sparkling and spectacular qualities that make certain other immortals vivid and endearing to the popular imagination. That is why any effort to preserve as many as possible of the small intimate contacts with the man whom historians and biographers have removed to Olympic heights, is extremely valuable. When we see in the glass case in the Masonic Temple the white gloves that covered those huge hands of his, the compass which he carried in his pocket as a young surveyor, the pruning-knife, worn by the pressure of his palm, the clock whose cords were cut at the moment of his death, he seems a little more of a human actuality to us.

The Masons are tremendously proud of Washington's connection with them and hope to dedicate the George Washington National Masonic Memorial Temple on his two hundredth anniversary in 1932. This gigantic temple, which is the most conspicuous thing in Alexandria from the railroad, stands upon Shooter's Hill — probably named after that Shooter's Hill in London which Dickens mentions in his 'Tale of Two Cities.' It was this site which was seriously considered by Madison and Jefferson for the National Capital. It had a commanding prospect, and the flourishing city of Alexandria could not imagine that she would ever be surpassed by Georgetown — which was the only part of the present Washington which then existed. But George Washington, who was President of the United States, was also a large landowner in Alexandria. He possessed tenements, property of various kinds, his own town mansion, and he was reluctant to take any public action which could possibly be construed as an aid to his private wealth. Therefore he decided to place the Nation's Capital on the opposite side of the Potomac.

George Washington was not the only figure

whose shadow still falls across the legends of Alexandria. These streets are lined with houses that were familiar to Lafayette, John Paul Jones, Aaron Burr, Fairfax, and John Marshall. Stablers-Leadbeater's Drug Store was the gathering-place of James Rumsey, who invented the first steamboat and who is buried in Westminster Abbey; George Mason, who drafted the Bill of Rights; George Johnson, who drafted the resolution nullifying the Stamp Act; Patrick Henry, John Randolph of Roanoke, and a score of other eager young patriots. Many of the houses are marked by bronze tablets, but many more, whose candles have lighted lineaments familiar to every school child, fold behind their unassuming front doors a host of household legends and personal anecdotes of men who are now almost fables in American history.

The family of Robert E. Lee has long been connected with the place. General Henry Lee — Light-Horse Harry — came in from Stratford, in Westmoreland County, in 1811, in order to educate his children. He occupied several houses, notably one at 611 Cameron Street, which is marked. This gentleman seems to have had a gift for phrases, judging from his own dashing sobriquet and his creation of the slogan, 'First in war, first

in peace, and first in the hearts of his countrymen.'
He was an intrepid soldier. Once, after he was
Governor of Virginia — an office which he held
three times — he resumed his generalship of Washington's Cavalry to put down the Whiskey Rebel-
lion. When he died, he left a young son, little
Robert E. Lee, whose mother carried him to live at
111 Orinoco Street — to the dignified house still
standing with its spacious side yard. This little
boy went to the Public Academy, then to the Hal-
lowell School, and was confirmed at Christ Church.
When he was a man it was in this church that he
stood after service conferring with the gentlemen
from Richmond who had come to offer him the
command of the Army of Virginia. This was, by
coincidence, the very spot where Washington had
stood consulting with his friends and advisers
as to whether he should break with the mother
country and become Commander-in-Chief of the
Colonial forces. And yet it was not entirely coincidence. Christ Church, so effectively set at the con-
junction of Cameron and Columbus Streets, was
the natural center of the community life. And like
so many of Alexandria's landmarks, it has been
admirably preserved.

Since 1773 it has stood very much as we see it

to-day, with its graveyard at the rear and its lovely spire outlined against the soft Virginia sky. Since 1773 the tablets on either side of the wineglass pulpit, lettered with the perfection of a medieval missal, have held their solemn injunctions before the eyes of the congregation. James Wren — a relative of Christopher's — is said to have been paid eight pounds for writing these tablets, and so flawlessly did he perform his task that there has been no need ever to retouch the gilt background or black letters. The organ came in 1810, the cutglass chandelier from England eight years later, at the same time that the tower was completed and the bell hung. Washington and Lee pews are both marked with silver plates. It is a completely satisfactory little church, the arched windows in the second story showing the thickness of the brick walls, and letting in the sunlight to rest upon the hand-carved paneling and the cornices of white pine. The weathered headstones in the graveyard testify to the democracy of death: two of Washington's pallbearers are there, Mrs. Ann Warner, a favorite actress of her generation, and the oldest inhabitant of this cheerful necropolis, Isaac Pearce, who has held the place of priority since 1771. Originally this was the town burying-ground, but

now an applicant for such interment must be a
church member, and quite properly so, for, although the living Alexandria may expand indef-
initely, this smaller permanent residential section
has immutable limits.

This living Alexandria still exists vitally on the
'Old Hill' where the Virginia Theological Seminary
and the famous Episcopal High School are seques-
tered. This seminary has played an unbroken rôle
in the ecclesiastical history of our country, and
many of our most eminent divines, including Phil-
lips Brooks, have received their education here.
The tourist who merely sees from a distance the
unfortunate pagoda-like tower of the main building can form no idea of the otherwise delightful
'Old Hill.' This startling excrescence was once ex-
plained to a visiting English cleric as having been
instigated by a dean who had been a missionary
to China. The visitor nodded thoughtfully — 'The
Chinese had their revenge.'

The most important residence in Alexandria is
Carlyle House, which was built in 1752 by a Scotch
merchant, John Carlyle, who had married into
the Fairfax family. A substantial building, erected
upon the site of an old fort, it is open to the public in its original furnishings — the fine mantels,

the carved four-post beds, the crystal candle wind-
shields, the well-rubbed fireside benches — all the
household equipment of a wealthy and dignified
Colonial home. General Braddock was permitted
to use it as headquarters during England's campaign against the aggression of the French in America. Benjamin Franklin, then Postmaster General,
consulted with him here about mail facilities, and
here later the Governors of the Five Colonies held a
conference, a conference which ultimately resulted
in the Stamp Act. Washington dined here frequently on both political and social occasions, for
this admirably run mansion was the social center of
pre-Revolutionary Alexandria. That social life was
no crude frontier affair, in spite of the newness of
the Colony. The refinement of the furnishings
testify not only to wealth, but to a standard of living and manners comparable to the best in con-
temporary London. Neither was Carlyle House an
isolated example. Gadsby's Tavern, the scene of
the famous Birthnight Balls for the King and
Queen and later of George Washington's Birthday
celebration, contained a ballroom so elegant that it
is at present in the Metropolitan Museum in New
York. The American Legion has now purchased
the old hostelry and intends to restore it as a me-

morial to Alexandria men who died in the Great War.

Inevitably many interesting places have been changed by time. Only the site exists of the Assembly Hall where Alexandrians met to consider and repudiate the Stamp Act, resolving that even 'if Boston is forced to submit we will not.' The jail, where French and Indian prisoners were held and where Jeremiah Moore was imprisoned for 'preaching the gospel without a license' (and freed by the fiery intervention of Patrick Henry), is also gone, along with George Mason's office and George Johnson's house, and the Academy of the First Free School. Marshall House, where the first drop of blood was shed in the war between the States, has been absorbed into indistinguishable walls, and the façade of the Alexandria *Gazette* — the oldest daily in America, having been published continuously since 1784 — looks very new. But should one of the inhabitants of Belle Haven, as Alexandria was originally called — return to-day he would see enough familiar landmarks to make him feel not wholly lost. He would recognize the gambrel roof of the little Ramsay House, the scene of much candlelighted hospitality during Colonial and Revotionary times; he would pass his hand over the admirable iron railing of that red-brick meeting-house which has tenaciously borne witness to Scotch Presbyterianism since 1774. He would learn that Rolling Road, used by the first settlers for literally rolling their hogsheads of tobacco down to market, was now the King's Highway. Perhaps in the manner of old people he would shake his head reproachfully at these alterations and then, his eyes turning to the end of the street, he would catch a white sail skimming up the river just as it might have done three centuries ago. And that fugitive glimpse would suddenly make it all clear and dear to him again, and he would know that he was still in Belle Haven, with its streets named for English royalty, and its architecture and its manners still reminiscent of its passionate kinship with the mother country.

Virginians have always preferred to live on their country estates, coming to the city or going abroad for a few months in the winter. Thus it was quite natural that, while George Washington kept his town house in Alexandria, he spent the greater part of the year at Mount Vernon, seven miles away. And it is Mount Vernon that we must now see.

Like Westminster Abbey, this national shrine

suffers from hackneyed description. School children and tourists are unceasingly herded through its grounds and corridors. Only one thing could lift it from this ruck of commonplaceness — its own sheer loveliness. Set with incomparable serenity high above the Potomac, surrounded by its outbuildings, gardens, lawns, and walks, it is flawless in design and in detail. And through some indestructible innate quality it does more than present a static picture of an ideal country estate. It curiously holds in its panelled rooms and in its box-bordered walks an atmosphere of gentility that no crowd can ruffle, no democratic jostling can sully.

When we were very small and were taken on a special occasion to call upon some formal relative, what an awe pervaded our childish breasts as we were ushered into the orderly and hushed hall! How inexpressibly serious the business was! How august even the least important personage connected with the establishment! There is only one place left in our disillusioned adulthood where this profoundly grown-up gravity still exists, and that is Mount Vernon. Other spots may fill us with greater reverence or greater exaltation. Saint Peter's is loftier, Versailles more elaborate, the Houses of Parliament more extensive. But nothing, no, nothing in the world is so irrefutably genteel as this simple white house with its pleasant lawn. Here is, in truth, George Washington's perpetual monument. The impeccable restoration, the exquisite maintenance of the place does, of course, contribute to its atmosphere of absolute perfection. But the secret is subtler. Every man's house is the extension of his personality. That is the secret of Mount Vernon.

CHAPTER II

FREDERICKSBURG AND THE OLD DOMINION

LEAVING Alexandria we begin our penetration of a State of about two and a half million people, ninety-seven per cent of whom are native-born, seven tenths of whom are white, and three fourths of whom live in the country. The children we meet trooping from school are either fair-haired, with Anglo-Saxon names, or chocolate-colored — and with the same Anglo-Saxon names. It is a cheerful and homogeneous society with none of the problems, either in classroom or factory, of unassimilable foreign immigration.

We are at the same time entering into that fasci-

nating region which, since 1650, has held the name
of the Old Dominion.

It is odd that so few people, even Virginians
themselves, know how the State came by this ap-
pellation, for it is based upon historical fact that is
easily accessible. The Cavaliers in Virginia were
united in their conviction that the execution of
Charles the First was nothing more nor less than
cold-blooded murder. So strongly did they feel
this that in October, 1649 — nine months after the
execution — the House of Burgesses passed a law
declaring that, if any one in Virginia said that the
execution of the 'late most excellent and now un-
doubtedly sainted king' was justifiable, such persons should be punished as traitors, precisely as if
they had taken part in the king's death. In this
law is a remarkable phrase referring to 'his sacred
majesty that now is,' and again it threatens with
bloody punishment any one who denies 'the inherent right of *his majesty that now is* to the colony
of Virginia.' This wording is comprehensible only
when we remember the royalist belief that the
moment one king dies, at that moment the next
heir begins to reign. It therefore refers to the son of
Charles the First, a weedy youth of eighteen, and
a fugitive in Holland. This good-natured, rather

worthless chap was declared by Virginia to be the true King of England, an announcement that no one in England itself — held in the stern grip of Cromwell — would have dared to breathe. Virginia, while being passionately loyal to the mother country, was equally passionate in the affirmation of her own independence. She snapped her fingers at Cromwell and actually sent off one of her prominent men, Colonel Richard Lee, to Breda, where he found young Charles and formally offered to make him King of Virginia — all of which was written down by William Lee, cousin of Richard and Sheriff of London. Charles politely declined the honor, but, in writing back to Governor Berkeley and giving that gentleman a new commission, he signed himself as Charles the Second, King of England. Virginia accepted this as a real commission from a real king. This was all very annoying to Cromwell, who in 1652 sent a fleet over to Jamestown to put an end to this nonsensical royalist business. There was no battle, but a summons to surrender to the authority of Parliament. Virginia accepted this summons in an amazing manner. She made terms precisely as if she were one nation treating with another. The paper still exists in which she declares that the Virginians were not 'forced nor constrained by a conquest of country' to surrender, but did so of their own accord. But they had no intention of being suppressed and intended to enjoy every privilege belonging to the English people. No man was to be punished for anything he had said or done in favor of the King. Virginia was to have the right of trading freely with all nations. Governor Berkeley was not to be interfered with or his property touched, and they were to be allowed to use the Episcopal prayerbook in church. These were a few of the terms! Cromwell was wise enough to make no objections. He realized that destroying Virginia would merely weaken England. In this way Virginia 'surrenders to the authority of Parliament.' Governor Berkeley retired to his plantation and the House of Burgesses went on making laws and governing the country as if it were an independent nation. When finally England did decide to place Charles the Second on the throne, Virginia pointed out that she had already proclaimed him King of Virginia. In fact, Virginia was his Old Dominion. It is said that at his coronation he wore a robe of Virginia silk to show his affection for these distant subjects, as it was engraved on coins that the English kingdom should henceforth consist of 'England, Scotland, Ireland, and Virginia.'

Certain it is that Fredericksburg was a town of ardent convictions. When she was royalist, she out-Englished the English. At the time of the Revolution she furnished arms and men and money with inexhaustible energy. From 1812 until 1864 she flung herself into the heyday of luxurious living — delighting in country mansions, race-courses, wine-cellars, and balls. During the war between the States she was literally riven asunder. And now, if she appears a little tired, who can blame her? For Fredericksburg is very old — much older than her legal birthday of 1671, when she was recognized as Leaseland by a grant from Sir William Berkeley, and older than 1727, when she received the charter from the House of Burgesses and was named Fredericksburg in honor of the Prince of Wales, son of George the Second. Her legend goes back to 1571, when Spanish missionaries are said to have erected here the first Christian shrine in America. While this is not absolutely authenticated, it is highly probable, for we do know that Spain made an effort to colonize Virginia very early. In 1526 a party of Spaniards came up the James River from Haiti, with six hundred people and many slaves. They founded the town of Miguel, where James-town now stands, and it is well within the bounds of probability that they came farther up to what is now Fredericksburg.

This dim picture of the past makes the existing landmarks seem almost modern. Kenmore, where Washington's only sister Betty Lewis lived, although built in 1752, is merely agreeably old-fashioned and not in the least decrepit, with its elaborately wrought stucco ceilings and overmantels, excellent stairway, brass locks, and crystal chandeliers. And the conservative frame house where his mother lived and died is quite up-to-date, comparatively speaking. It is Mary Washington, associated with Fredericksburg for her widowhood of nearly half a century, who has been made the chief historical heroine of the place. One may see her brick-floored kitchen and her sewing-stand in the plain rooms where she passed those years which seem quite uneventful except for the occasional visits of her son; one may see the monument erected to her — the only one given by women to a woman; one may read among the records in the Courthouse the meticulously worded will in which she apportions her 'purple cloth cloak lined with shay' to one relative, 'a blanket and a pair of sheets' to another, and so forth. Everything this composed old lady in the white apron dealt with, she apparently left

in admirable order, including her children and her
receipt for gingerbread.

There is no lack of historic spots, well marked, in
the city. The long one-storied brick building which
President Monroe used as a law office; the now
shabby wooden house which he once owned; the
slave block on Commerce Street; Rising Sun Tavern, built by George Washington's brother Charles,
and once the gathering-spot for Revolutionists who
drafted here the resolution — which they later
passed in town meeting — tantamount to a Declaration of Independence. There is the Courthouse
with its records, the statue of General Mercer, and
his remodeled home, the Sentry Box, which served
as a signal station during three wars.

But the charm of Fredericksburg is not primarily
along its streets, but lies, rather, in its estates —
plantations, some of them a score of miles away,
and still claiming Fredericksburg as an address.
Stratford, the ancient home of the Lees, was built
by a 'bountiful present from the privy purse' of the
Queen of England. Wakefield, where Washington
was born, and Epping Forest, his mother's birthplace, Mount Airey, the home of the Tayloes, are
only a few of the many of gentle tradition. Gunston
Hall — nearer Washington than Fredericksburg —

is charmingly restored and adorned with the boxwood planted two centuries ago, and the town of
Falmouth, which the average tourist never heard of
until he crossed its borders, was a far more important center than Fredericksburg in the early
days. The first flour mill in America stood here,
and Basil Gordon, who made his money by shipping flour and tobacco directly from his own private
wharf to England, bringing back bricks as ballast,
was the first American millionaire. This delight-
fully preserved town served as a grain market for
the upper country and traded directly with Europe
and the West Indies, and its wharves were crowded
with deep-sea vessels.

Of all the beautiful estates in the vicinity of
Fredericksburg, perhaps Chatham is the most
felicitous example, as its plans were drawn by Sir
Christopher Wren, and it still stands, after two
hundred years, in perfect preservation. It rises in
wooded terraces from the Rappahannock and with
an extended view of the spires and roofs of Fredericksburg. A sun-drenched mansion, splendid and
yet unpretentious, overlooking a lawn with col-
umned summer house, and gardens edged with box
or enclosed by brick walls topped by pineapple
decorations. It has always been the home of people

CHATHAM, A SUN-DRENCHED MANSION, SPLENDID AND YET UNPRETENTIOUS

who have loved it, and its last owners have preserved its original dignity while skillfully extending its garden, guest-house, pools, and pheasant runs. Standing under the well-kept trees, the boxwood pungent in our nostrils, it is easy to imagine the beauty of living which has passed before these walls, from which the whitewashing, flecking off, reveals the soft rosy speckle of the bricks below. Washington has stayed here; Lee courted his wife beneath these trees; Madison, Monroe, Washington Irving, Lincoln have stood where we are standing, looking out over the grassed terraces across the river to the town. A house like this needs no argument to explain its merit. It is thought that William Pitt, Earl of Chatham, commissioned Wren to draw the plans and then presented them to William FitzHugh, who had been his classmate at Eton and Oxford and was then living in Virginia. FitzHugh named the place for his friend, and, although it has passed through other hands since then, it still retains its name of Chatham.

It is houses like this — and the countryside around Fredericksburg is particularly rich in them — which marked the apex of happy and luxurious Southern living, and houses like this which were sacked and destroyed during the fearful conflict between North and South. Mahogany furniture was splintered into firewood: portraits ripped by bayonets, silver stolen and porcelain smashed. It is not strange that certain families cannot even now quite forget all they have lost. For if Fredericksburg escaped the depredations of the Revolution — for although she gave generously of men and arms she was physically untouched — she was the most lamentable victim of the war between the States. Halfway between Washington and Richmond, she was the natural objective for both Northern and Southern troops. Fought over, shelled, evacuated, reoccupied, and ravaged, she suffered more disastrously perhaps than any other city. All about her stretch the rows of her cemeteries and the scenes of battles. Along the desolate Wilderness Road granite blocks with bronze plaques state that here the battle of Chancellorsville was fought, with the loss of thirty thousand men. A little farther on, the battle of the Wilderness, with twenty-nine thousand lost. At Spottsylvania Court House twenty-nine thousand were annihilated. Including the battle of Fredericksburg one hundred and six thousand men were killed within this comparatively limited area — which is horrifying even to a generation used to the figures of the Great War. Monuments

are here, too: one where Stonewall Jackson received
— accidentally from his own men — the shot that
mortally wounded him. It is profoundly depressing
to follow this road, remembering the agonies of the
campaigns fought over this terrain.

Fredericksburg clings to its past. It points out
the place where John Paul Jones lived for a while,
the home of William Fontaine Maury, and the site
of the house of Captain William Lewis Herndon,
the first explorer of the Amazon. But in spite of
its tenaciously maintained traditions, Fredericksburg is not exempt from the universal law of change.
Some of the beautiful old plantation houses are in
the hands of strangers: one of the most famous of all
— Smithfield — is a country club. On Marye's
Heights, crowned with artillery on that fatal thirteenth of December in 1863, is now the State
Normal School. The old hotels and inns for which
the town was noted in the days when it was on the
main line of travel between North and South, have
been torn down, remodeled, forgotten. The steam-
boats and the railroads, carrying their own dining-
room and sleeping accommodations, gave these
hostelries their death blow. Now only a few of the
picturesque names are even remembered.

Fredericksburg is still beloved by hundreds of

Southern families who trace back to her their beginnings and their ancestral homes, and to hundreds of newer arrivals who have chosen to live within a pleasant radius of her domain. But the stranger who visits her for the first time is chiefly conscious that beneath his feet on every side lie graveyards; that mansions which once vibrated with life are now museums, and that the long Wilderness Road is too sorrowfully set with tragic markers.

As we leave the old city for Richmond, we touch Spottsylvania County, where Virginia tried her first experiment with foreign labor. It was Governor Spotswood who discovered iron ore deposits on his great grant of land, and had a colony of Germans brought over from Müsen, Westphalia, where they had learned their trade in an iron mine which has been continuously worked since the early part of the fourteenth century. The skilled laborers which he imported laid the foundation for the iron and steel industry in this country, and Spotswood's nickname of the 'Tubal-Cain of America' has proved entirely appropriate. The spot where these aliens made their home was called Germanna, and they stayed there until 1720. Then, owing to some difference with Governor Spotswood, they moved to

what is now Fauquier County, and settled nine
miles south of Warrenton, naming their new settlement Germantown. This was over two centuries
ago. Since then Virginia has been content to use its
own native-born laborers who manage to make a
cheerful competence without bothering about labor
unions or the problems of unemployment. In fact
the strenuous tourist, glancing at the chatting
groups on the doorsteps, or whirling past an occasional unhurrying figure on the road, wonders, a
little enviously, if the necessity for any employ-
ment at all is not a matter of regret to a large number of leisure-loving folk of the Old Dominion.

CHAPTER III

RICHMOND, THE CONFEDERATE CAPITAL

RICHMOND — the city of historic tradition, the jealous conservator of prejudice and pride, the beautiful ancient capital, seated on its seven hills beside the river — the stranger who comes to see these oft-sung glories will get hardly more of them than the passenger on an ocean liner may glimpse of the intricate life on the floor of the sea. For Richmond to-day is, to superficial glance, a modern city with handsome railroad stations, hotels, department stores, factories, and parks. Apartment houses with shiny new roofs line the

boulevards, and 'residential areas' and suburbs
are sprouting with English manor houses, Italian
villas, and Dutch Colonial cottages. New churches
and expensive antique shops waylay the tentative
explorer on every corner, but he will have to search
vigilantly and in unfashionable districts for the
oldest Masonic Hall in America, and he will have
to travel even farther to find Saint John's Church.

But although Richmond is overlaid with a thick
coat of modernity, one must not conclude that it is
therefore a modern city. Behind certain ugly and
substantial brownstone fronts, behind the calm
façades of certain lofty mansions, and in uncounted
single rooms in shabby boarding-houses on obscure
streets, the old code, the old passions, and the old
memories still persist. But for the stranger within
the gates to jump in and order a prompt draught of
that peculiar blend of complacency and charm
which has always characterized this unique community — he might as well expect the Pope to
hurry over and slap him on the back when he is
admitted to the Vatican. Richmond is still the
sacred repository of Southern memories and of
many tangible Southern souvenirs. But as befits
old and dignified persons and places, it does not
reveal its heart at the first chance encounter. Per-

haps no one who has not been born in Richmond can ever be admitted into the holy of holies which in this case has always demanded a social rather than a financial abracadabra — although it is now regretfully admitted that wealth, when properly combined with other qualifications, is not entirely imponderable.

The tourist, even though thus thrust into outer darkness, need not, however, consume his time by gnashing his teeth, but may, on the contrary, put in a very enjoyable day. For delightful as the aroma of exclusive aristocracy undeniably is, and seriously as it is guarded by its proprietors, there are in Richmond sufficient attractions of national rather than provincial importance to satisfy any not-too-grasping seeker after entertainment.

First of all he must see the James River — that memorable waterway which created the distinctive civilization of Tidewater Virginia, setting it definitely apart from the rest of the State. Like the Thames and the Tiber, it is not at first sight particularly impressive. It is shallow and tortuous and rather yellow. But pausing on the wide and busy bridge which spans it, we remember that nine days after the landing at Jamestown and thirteen years before the landing of the Pilgrim fathers at

Plymouth, Captain Newport and Captain John
Smith and a party of men ascended the James River
and discovered the site of the present city of Richmond. The first view that Englishmen had of the
spot is thus graphically and poetically set down by
John Smith in his 'True Relations,' which was
printed in London in 1608. He says: ' . . . we passed
on further where within an ile [mile] we were inter-
rupted with great craggy stones in the midst of the
river, where the water falleth so rudely and with
such violence that not any boat can possibly passe,
and so broad disperseth the streame as there is not
past five or sixe foote at low water, and to the shore
scarce passage with a barge.' In the journal of
Colonel William Evelyn Byrd for September 19,
1773, we read, 'When we got home we laid the
foundations for two large cities — one at Schoccos,
to be called Richmond.'

Colonel Byrd, ancestor of the present Governor
of the State, and of Commander Richard Evelyn
Byrd, was one of the most intellectual men that
Virginia was to know. Among other services to
the civilization of the new world he contributed the
largest library that had been brought across the
ocean, the ineffably lovely house of Westover, which
is still one of the show places of the South, and a

daughter Evelyn, who died of a broken heart, thereby furnishing a theme congenial to poets and novelists ever since. Yes, one must assuredly start with the James River and the Byrds before setting forth to see Richmond.

Of Colonial Richmond little remains in literature or in reality. Saint John's Church on Church Hill (originally Richmond Hill) is the most complete memento. The oldest part was built in 1740, and the fluted bowl of Virginia limestone, which is now used as a baptismal font, is said to be three hundred years old, and was once stolen by the Indians and used for grinding corn. At one time this was the only church and the largest public building in the city, and in it were held political meetings — notably the Virginia Convention of 1775 at which Patrick Henry demanded liberty or death. Inside these white clapboarded walls Benedict Arnold quartered his troops, and outside of them are many memorable graves, including that of George Wythe, a signer of the Declaration of Independence.

But it is the war between the States rather than the Revolution of which one is most keenly aware in Richmond. And this awareness is intensified by the Confederate flags flying on either side of Battle Abbey — that handsome repository for paintings, statuary, portraits of Confederate statesmen and heroes, and books of reference for the future historian. In the south room of the building, Charles Hoffbauer, the French artist, has distinguished himself by some admirable mural paintings of Civil War scenes. He had just begun his work when the Great War broke out and he returned to his native country of France and fought for five years. Then he came back to Richmond and completed the murals in two years — with a far more emotionalizing comprehension of the tragedy of war than if the interruption had not occurred.

The collection of paintings in the north room was given by the Honorable John Barton Payne, Secretary of the Interior in President Wilson's Cabinet. The Judge was a loyal Virginian, and the collection is one of the worthiest in the South.

Impressive as Battle Abbey is, it lacks the touching intimacy which characterizes the White House of the Confederacy — that building which was associated with so many domestic as well as public events during those tragic years. Here Jefferson Davis lived, and his daughter Winnie was born. Here his little son died. Lincoln's son, it will be remembered, died in the same period and the two fathers exchanged letters of sympathy. The man-

sion also served as General Lee's war-time house,
and has set aside a separate room for each of the
Confederate States. These memorial chambers hold
the worn uniforms and faded letters, the swords
and money and tattered flags of the Lost Cause.

The Valentine Museum sounds the same sad
note, although it hopes soon to become a somewhat
different type of domestic museum by restoring
the house, with its spiral stair, good woodwork,
and carved white marble mantels, to its original
elegance.

The most historical section of the city is the
Capitol Square, with the old gray bell-tower where
the alarm was sounded when the Federal troops
were about to enter Richmond after seven days'
fighting; with the Governor's house, the oldest and
most perfect in the United States, and with the
Capitol building whose plans Jefferson himself
furnished. It was when he was Minister to France
that he fell in love, as he wrote home, not with a
woman, but with a building — the Maison Carrée
at Nîmes. And upon the lines of the Maison Carrée
the new Capitol at Richmond was modeled, and
its corner-stone laid in 1785. When the wings were
added later, they were designed to harmonize with
the original. A building so old as this in a city so

important is inevitably packed with associations. Here in the Hall of the House of Delegates was held part of the trial of Aaron Burr. Here met the Constitutional Convention of 1829–30, and also the Secession Convention of 1861, and subsequent sessions of the Confederate Congress. In the State Land Office are records of land grants going back as far as 1623. In the Rotunda is Houdon's statue of Washington — the only one for which he ever posed, and declared by Lafayette to be a perfect likeness. The equestrian statue in the grounds, surrounded by heroic figures, is by Crawford.

The whole Capitol Square is admirably situated and laid out, and as dignified and pleasing as any in the United States.

Another building peculiarly precious to Richmond is Monumental Church, for it stands upon ground that has been significant in local affairs since 1756, when Monsieur Quesnay, an enthusiastic Frenchman, built upon it a frame house in which he established an academy. He had the most ambitious plans for developing this into a university, but the plans fell through and the assembly hall became a playhouse. Here was held the Convention of 1789, which ratified the Constitution of the United States, then hanging in the balance and

needing Virginia's voice to save it from defeat. The
first Assembly Theater was destroyed by fire and
succeeded by another, the Richmond Theater,
where many well-known actors and actresses —
including Elizabeth Arnold Poe, the mother of the
poet — played in Placide's Stock Company. It was
this Richmond Theater which went up most hor-
ribly in flames one night during a performance,
killing seventy-three persons including the Governor of the State and injuring scores of others. The
holocaust made a terrific sensation throughout the
entire country. The members of the United States
Senate wore crêpe armbands for a month. Every
one in Richmond was dressed in mourning for
thirty days. All entertainments and balls were
prohibited for four months, and the city purchased
the theater site and decided that the memorial
should take the form of a 'Monumental Church
to be forever kept sacred for the purpose of divine
worship.' This spot is not only associated with loss
in many Richmond families, but it was also for
many years the most fashionable church in the city.
John Marshall attended here, unlatching the pew-
door when he knelt down, to make room for his
long legs in the aisle. Lafayette and other distinguished visitors came here. And here often sat

John Allan, the shrewd Scotch merchant with his lovely wife, and their small adopted son with wide gray eyes and delicate long curls beneath a purple cap with a gold tassel.

It is to this child more than to any other single figure that the city owes its fame in the outer world. Richmond herself, perhaps, does not entirely realize this. She is proudly and constantly conscious of having been the former capital of the Confederacy and of being the present capital of the State of Virginia. But in countries where American intestine wars are only faintly remembered and in cities where the subtleties of Southern politics are only vaguely apprehended, there are people who, scanning the literary sky which arches over all the civilized world, see there Edgar Allan Poe as America's brightest star.

Poe was not born in Richmond, although he always associated himself with it in his own mind. This skyey-eyed child was born in Boston. He was, however, taken to Richmond at an early age, and there his mother, a young and widowed actress, died in extreme poverty and was buried in the graveyard of Saint John's Church. The extraordinarily beautiful little boy, with the gray eyes and the soft dark hair, was adopted — although not legally — by

Mrs. Frances Allan, the childless wife of a well-to-do Scotch merchant. His early years were protected by the utmost tenderness of his adoptive mother and aunt, by kindness from John Allan and by every comfort and privilege. He went to Scotland and England with the Allans and was put in good schools there. He came back with them to Richmond and shared like a son in the luxurious great house which John Allan — with recently inherited wealth — now purchased. This mansion may still be seen, as may the house where 'Helen' lived — Mrs. Stanard.

Reared to the lavish standards befitting a Virginia gentleman, with a taste for fastidious dress and living, spoiled perhaps by the excessive devotion of the women of the household, Poe was not, however, legally adopted by John Allan, for reasons which have long intrigued biographers and psychoanalysts.

He was sent to the University of Virginia, where he stayed only a year, as his foster-father refused to pay his debts — debts which were inevitably incurred, since his allowance was below his strictest necessities. At this period students came to the University of Virginia with tandems of blooded horses, with servants and pointers and sets of dueling pistols. It was a dashing and fashionable place, and Poe, who had been brought up to consider himself as a member of this aristocracy, was supposed to hold his place with it with a dole insufficient to cover the bare tuition charges. Proud and furious, he set himself to meet his bills by gambling and ended by finding himself in deeper disaster. John Allan's cruel and arbitrary action in so suddenly cutting down the lad whom he had brought up to expect a son's rights, and Poe's own peculiar and supersensitive characteristics, constitute one of the most spectacular tragedies in the history of letters. It is the conflict between two natures — the older one shrewd, hard, and carnal, the younger one compact of egotism, fiery genius, and utter impracticality. The terrific struggle ended in an agony which shattered the poet's nervous system and released an inspired utterance not yet surpassed by the tongue of mortal man.

Poe is associated with many places besides Richmond. He lived in New York, in Philadelphia, in Baltimore, in Fordham. But he always considered himself a Virginian from Richmond. It was here that his childhood, boyhood, and early youth were spent: here was the scene of later triumphs and defeats, and here the Edgar Allan Poe Shrine has been created.

In the oldest house in the city, so old that it is the only one known where 'J R' for Jacobus Rex may still be traced upon one of the stones, a small rock building, which was used by Washington as his headquarters, is collected what is left of the few earthly possessions of Edgar Allan Poe. Here is the small battered trunk which held his manuscripts and the shabby tag ends of his diminishing wardrobe. Here is the broken key to it which was found in his pocket after he died. Here are the handsome decanters and substantial dining-room table at which he sat when being brought up as the only son of the wealthy merchant. And close by, in mute contrast, is the humble brass ladle that was part of the last meager equipment of Fordham. Here is a cheap little red trinket box, all we have left of Virginia, the child wife whose blood relationship to him and whose mortal malady so poignantly affected her husband's imagination. Here are two of the painted chairs, purchased in a brief interval of prosperity by poor Maria Clemm to keep life together for her beloved daughter and equally adored son-in-law. Those painted chairs, bought with the ineradicable feminine instinct to make a home, given up with what despair as part payment of the rent — how they represent the selfless life of

THE EDGAR ALLAN POE HOUSE, RICHMOND

Maria Clemm heartbrokenly interwoven with that of Poe! A letter from her — her last — asking certain relations for money with which she may go South to end her days in a home that has been offered, is one of the most dignified and touching documents in the whole cabinet of manuscripts whose value is beyond computation. Some of the narrow blue manuscripts are pasted together to form a long roll — Virginia's pathetic contribution to usefulness. The very meagerness of these mementoes is inexpressibly affecting. In their scantiness, in their painful starkness they testify to the only contact with reality that was vouchsafed the man who wrote so hypnotizingly of velvet cushions and floating draperies and tessellated floors.

Alexandria, Fredericksburg, and Richmond are the only glimpses of Tidewater Virginia we shall see on this trip. That fascinating region, so distinct from any other part of the State, evolved its own architecture and its own culture and demands a trip — and a book — to itself.

We must now strike west and north, toward the lesser-known Piedmont Virginia — that high plateau stretching from the Potomac and Maryland line southwest two hundred and forty-four miles, to the banks of the Dan at the North Carolina boundary.

Part II
THROUGH PIEDMONT VIRGINIA

CHAPTER IV

THE TOWN OF CHARLOTTESVILLE

THE town of Charlottesville, in the approximate center of Albemarle County, is admirably situated as a headquarters in which to settle down for a long or a short stay and from which to make various trips throughout Virginia. It is, perhaps, rather dangerously so, for it appears to be populated, to a considerable extent, by people who came for a night, decided to rent a house, and then to buy or build one, and who are still living there, after thirty or forty years. But this Circe has a knack of transforming her visitors into far comelier shapes than their original ones. The dyspeptic New-Englander, the hustling Westerner, and the money-conscious New-Yorker are all enchanted, after a few seasons, into a gentler and a gayer semblance.

Charlottesville was made the county seat of Albemarle in 1762 and was named in honor of the little Princess Charlotte of Mecklenburg-Strelitz, the young bride of George the Third. It lies about four hundred feet above sea level in the Blue Ridge foothills and has some secret pact with Apollo, whereby it receives more sunshine of a superfine quality than almost any other spot on the globe. When the sunshine is turned off, the moonlight is turned on. And a shorn lamb is perpetually tethered in a strategic point, judging from the carefully tempered wind.

Besides being the home of the most beautiful university in America, the town itself is distinguished by some surprisingly excellent statues. Each is effectively set off in a well-planted square commemorating not only the bronze-embodied heroes, but also Paul Goodloe McIntire, the idealistic private citizen who contributed them to the town where he was born and where he is still living.

CHARLOTTESVILLE, DISTINGUISHED BY SOME SURPRIS-
INGLY EXCELLENT STATUES

The finest of these is almost directly opposite the Monticello Hotel, and is by Charles Keck. It represents Stonewall Jackson, leaning slightly forward on his gallant 'Little Sorrel,' and is a work of such striking verve and spirit that it ranks, justly and absolutely, among the noblest equestrian statues in the world. The one of Robert E. Lee on 'Traveler' was begun by the late H. M. Schrady and finished after his death by Leo Lentelli. Magnificently placed, on the square that bears its name, it strikes that note which grows both stronger and sweeter with time. Robert E. Lee possessed the peculiarly endearing quality of bravery linked with gentleness: of personal charm with character. He still seems to win not only a place of honor but of tenderness in the hearts of all who learn about him, and it is appropriate that he should stand thus in the center of a Virginia town like Charlottesville.

The public library facing Lee Square is a gift from the same generous source and the work of Walter Dabney Blair. It is one of the most exquisite small libraries in the South.

Halfway between the center of the town and the University is a small square — Midway Park it is called — bearing the Lewis and Clark Memorial by Charles Keck. The statue with its three bronze figures, one of them Sacajawea, the Indian squaw who served as a guide, with its illustrative reliefs on the high granite pedestal, is worthy of the two men whom it commemorates — Meriwether Lewis and William Clark, both born in this vicinity. It is worthy, too, of that expedition which was one of the most valuable and extraordinary in the annals of our country.

Before the Louisiana Purchase, but while it was under his astute consideration, Jefferson began turning over in his mind plans for a scientific expedition which should explore that vast and only vaguely apprehended domain. He wanted to know more about its geographical characteristics and material resources, and as early as 1792 he proposed to the American Philosophical Society of Philadelphia the sending out of an exploring party with funds raised by subscription. The Sunday supplements and novels of to-day have a way of implying that scientific exploration originated with William Beebe, and spectacular flights into the unknown are a specialty of Charles Lindbergh. But the excitement of discovery and the calm and intelligent appraisal of the data it brings forth have fired enlightened minds in centuries before our own. Jefferson's interest in natural history was as eager

as Roosevelt's. It was once said that he and
Agassiz had done more for science in America than
any other two men, 'not so much by their direct
contribution to knowledge as by the immense
weight which they gave to scientific interests by
their advocacy.' Although the Louisiana Territory
still belonged to France, Jefferson decided that that
country would not object to a penetration which he
characteristically called 'a literary pursuit.' However, he kept his plans more or less secret while he
decided that the best man he could find to lead this
'pursuit' would be his secretary — Meriwether
Lewis. This young man had been with him two
years, and was, in Jefferson's words, 'brave, pru-
dent, habituated to the woods and familiar with
Indian manners and character.' 'He is not regularly educated,' Jefferson further wrote, 'but he
possesses a great mass of accurate information on
all subjects of nature which present themselves
here, and will therefore readily select those only
in his new route which shall be new.'

In order to acquire 'a greater familiarity with
the technical language of the natural sciences, and
readiness in the astronomical observations necessary for the geography of his route,' young Lewis
went up to Philadelphia, the principal seat of

learning in the country at that time, and studied under eminent scientists. Then, with Jefferson's approval, he chose his own associate, William Clark, his friend and companion in the campaigns under General Wayne. The two men supplemented each other admirably. Lewis was the more poetic and scholarly: Clark the more incisive. Their friendship was generous and enduring. Both shared equally in the perils and in the rewards of their great adventure. Their story, accurately given in the journals of each of them, is one of the most illuminating documents in the history of our country. Scientists in every field still refer to it.

In order to evaluate this superb undertaking, we must realize that up to this time none of the territory west of the Mississippi had been explored. The dividing lines between it and British America on the north and Mexico on the south were undefined. The country where the Missouri River had its source had never been entered by white men. The extent of the Rockies was not guessed at. They had been mapped in British America under the name of 'Stonies.'

After the signing of the treaty in May, 1803, the preparations were pushed forward with open activity. In June, Lewis and Clark set out. It is impossible in a book of this size even to outline the extraordinary scope and personnel of the party. Although the most valuable contribution was scientific, as Jefferson had foreseen, officially the expedition was a military one, and organized as such under the Secretary of War. In the bas-reliefs on the pedestal of the monument may be seen some of the soldiers and frontiersmen, French and half-breed *voyageurs* and interpreters, and Clark's negro servant.

Surmounting and leading them all are the two eager young men. Meriwether Lewis was twenty-nine and William Clark four years his senior, and they were the first explorers to reach the Pacific by crossing the continent north of Mexico. Their sufferings and triumphs, their buffalo chases and forays and conferences with the Indians — one of which gave its name to Council Bluffs — everything they saw and did was scrupulously recorded. Jefferson had been explicit in his injunction that all data must be written 'with great pains and accuracy, to be entered distinctly and intelligently for others as well as yourself.' Not only the two principals, but four of the sergeants and a number of the privates were fired with the ambition to record their experiences. They carried field notebooks in their pockets and at night developed the rough sketches and maps into more exact records. Besides these sketches of birds and fishes and leaves, observations on meteorology, geology, astronomy, and ethnology, Lewis sent the President sixty-one specimens of earth, salt, and minerals, and sixty specimens of plants.

It is interesting to remark that the value of these records was fully appreciated by the men themselves. Three days after they had returned to St. Louis, after an absence of more than two years of a 'gigantic Odyssey besides which the wandering Greeks were timid and provincial,' they began putting their data into definite literary form. Owing to difficulties with publishers and printers and the premature death of Lewis, the entire material was not properly edited and published until Dr. Reuben Gold Thwaites did it in 1904. Nevertheless the two explorers received full recognition. Although Lewis died at thirty-five, he lived long enough to enjoy the governorship of the Missouri Territory. William Clark lived to be sixty-eight, and held many high military and governmental offices. He died full of honors, at the home of his eldest son, Meriwether Lewis Clark.

It is a remarkably satisfactory story from beginning to end. The country was intelligently studied; the explorers were liberally rewarded, and their findings are properly before the public. Their friendship was altruistic, neither striving for prominence over the other. In fact, so closely did they deliberately ally themselves that even their names have become almost one name in the State of their birth, where their united statues stand looking west toward the country of their conquest.

In tragic contrast to this happily consummated enterprise stands another statue, near the east gate of the University, executed by Robert Aitken and presented, as were the other three, by Paul Goodloe McIntire. This is the memorial to George Rogers Clark, an older brother of William, and a man whose personality has never been popularly recognized, and whose services to his country have never been properly appreciated.

Even those of us whose historical memories are extremely sketchy know something about Lewis and Clark. How many of us realize that, if it had not been for the passionate military genius of George Rogers Clark, the entire country northwest of the Ohio River, which is now divided into Ohio, Indiana, Illinois, Michigan, Wisconsin, and part of Minnesota, would still belong to Great Britain?

Up to the eve of the American Revolution it was part of the British province of Quebec. She had acquired it from France by the Treaty of 1763 after Wolfe's victory on the Plains of Abraham. If George Rogers Clark had not conquered it before the Revolution, after the Revolution it would have remained as part of Quebec. No 'literary pursuit' this — but a conquest of blood and brawn. The story of this stirring and tragic figure was brilliantly summarized by Dr. Archibald Henderson at the unveiling of the Memorial in 1921. He said:

'George Rogers Clark was the most dynamic military figure of the Revolution. At the age of twenty-three, by force of sheer hardihood, he seized the military control of Kentucky. Under the veiled threat of leading in a revolution the rude borderers of the West, he dragooned Patrick Henry and the Virginia Council into furnishing the Kentucky stations with the indispensable ammunition for their defense. By ousting from the position of leadership Colonel Richard Henderson, President of the Colony of Transylvania, he virtually assumed the military dictatorship of the West. With the aid and countenance of Jefferson, Mason, and Wythe, he secretly and sagaciously projected a military expedition against the loosely held posts of the enemy in the Northwest; and personally conducted against Kaskaskia, Cahokia, and Vincennes a brilliant and meteoric campaign which was crowned with shining success. In the capture and retention of the fortified posts of Illinois, he made possible the diplomacy of Jay by which the boundary of the United States at the close of the Revolution was triumphantly pushed to the Lakes in the North and to the Mississippi on the West.

'When Clark achieved the capture of Hamilton at Vincennes in 1779, his star was at its zenith. Later years witnessed its progressive decline and tragic setting. He was ruined in fortune as the result of pledging his personal credit for the colossal expense of his arduous campaigns. This debt of honor incurred by Clark in behalf of Virginia was not settled by that great State until years after his death. He was embittered in spirit because Virginia gave him only a second-hand sword for his conquest of the Northwest, and relieved him of his military commission at the close of the Revolution. He slowly sank into the quicksands of inebriety; sullied his honor by selling his military services to a foreign power; and like Burr, Blount, and Wilkinson dallied with projects verging upon treason. Sunk to a mere shadow of his former greatness,

Clark went to his grave, unwept, unhonored, and unsung.

'Had Clark marched straight for Detroit after his capture of Hamilton at Vincennes, he might well have vied with Washington himself in military glory. Had Virginia heeded his oft-repeated pleas, promptly arranged the settlement of his accounts, and procured him a general's commission in the Continental Army, Clark might well have achieved national recognition in his lifetime and died with the plaudits of a grateful people ringing in his ears. "I have given the United States half the territory they possess," he wrote in 1792, "and for them to suffer me to remain in poverty in consequence of it, will not redound much to their honor hereafter."

'It is often the fate of great leaders, in America as elsewhere, to feel the sting of ingratitude at the hands of the people and the nation they have most unselfishly served. Washington, Lincoln, Grant, Roosevelt, Wilson — all suffered the reverses of popular opinion, a diminution of popularity and prestige.'

The lamentable weaknesses of Clark's own character in part explain the tragedy of his life; but it was what he felt to be the indifference and ingratitude of his country which soured and embittered his last years. It is said that, in a fit of black dejection induced by the continued failure of Virginia to settle his accounts, Clark thrust into the ground the second-hand sword Virginia had sent him in 1779, and broke it with his crutch.

In 1781, Virginia fittingly voted a resolution of thanks to Clark and his men, and generously donated to them one hundred and fifty thousand acres of land. With a belated recognition of the inadequacy of the second-hand sword of 1779, Virginia, thirty-three years later, voted Clark the pension of one half the full pay which he received as Colonel of the Illinois regiment, and a first-class sword manufactured at the armory of the State. In accepting this sword from General Mercer, Clark, the broken old conqueror of the Northwest — paralyzed, one leg gone, mind clouded with sorrow and drink — is reported to have said: 'You have made a very handsome address, and the sword is very handsome too. When Virginia needed a sword, I gave her one. I am too old and infirm, as you see, ever to use a sword again, but I am glad that my old mother State has not entirely forgotten me, and I thank her for the honor and you for your kindness and friendly words. . . .'

Three miles from Charlottesville is a rough

granite boulder upon a cement base. Upon it is a
bronze tablet, set there in 1925 by the Albemarle
Chapter of the Daughters of the American Revolution to commemorate the approximate birthplace
of the hero of Vincennes. It is easy to miss this
boulder, inconspicuously placed near the entrance
to Buena Vista. And it is possible to inquire of
half a dozen passers-by as to its location and to
have them dubiously shake their heads. They
never saw the bronze marker: they never heard of
George Rogers Clark. But once, hunting for it, a
Northern tourist met, in the autumn evening, an
old negro astride a nag, his trousers flapping with
the jogging trot. He stopped and politely listened
to the query. 'Yas, sah — yas, sah. It's right up
yonder — that memory stone'; and he pointed
through the gathering shadows. A memory stone!
For after one hundred and seventy-three years the
birthplace of Albemarle's most courageous son, who
won more territory than Napoleon or Alexander the
Great, was awarded recognition.

If George Rogers Clark and his epic conquest
were long unsung, there is another dashing hero of
Charlottesville who has not yet been sung at all,
outside local limits. This is Jack Jouett, who swept
through a performance far more spectacular and

important than Paul Revere's own. Paul Revere galloped fifteen miles over comparatively good roads to warn some private citizens of the approach of the British. Jack Jouett covered forty-five miles of the roughest conceivable terrain and saved the Governor of the State of Virginia and the Legislature itself.

As we return to the Monticello Hotel, we see almost directly opposite us the Red Land Club. On its front wall is affixed a tablet which reads:

Site of the Old Swan Tavern
Where lived and died Jack Jouett
Whose heroic ride saved
Mr. Jefferson the Governor
And the Virginia Assembly
From Capture by Tarleton
June 1781

Erected by the Monticello Branch
of the Association for
The Preservation of Virginia Antiquities
1910

Lord Cornwallis had sent Lieutenant-Colonel Tarleton to Charlottesville to seize Thomas Jefferson, who was Governor, and to disperse the Legislature. This Legislature contained no less than three signers of the Declaration of Independence, one of them the ancestor of two Presidents, and Patrick Henry. It was no mean covey Tarleton was to net. As for Jefferson, he was to be captured, fettered, transported to England, and doubtless executed for treason. Colonel Tarleton set forth with spirit. He had a hundred and eighty of his own best dragoons and seventy mounted infantry. He reached the Cuckoo Tavern in Louisa County, about fifty miles from Charlottesville, one fine June evening.

It happened that Jack Jouett, proprietor of the Swan Tavern in Charlottesville, was at the Cuckoo and saw Tarleton pass with his men. Instantly he divined his intention and its immense significance. He leaped on his horse and started for Monticello. Tarleton went by the road, Jack Jouett took an unfrequented back trail. It was a terrific ride, winding among the hills, obstructed by rocks and fallen trees and netted across by interlacing vines that tore his face so deeply that he bore the scars until he died. He started a little before midnight and at dawn the next morning he arrived in Milton, the little village at the ford, just below Monticello, where in after years Jefferson received the marble columns for the Rotunda. Jouett flew up the hill to Monticello, gave his warning, and tore down to Charlottesville to warn the Assembly, which promptly departed for Staunton. Ten minutes after Jefferson had left Monticello, the British reached it. It is almost impossible to estimate the result to our United States if Jefferson had been captured at this time. For this was at the very beginning of his long constructive labor for 'peace, prosperity, for the advancement of the people, for religious liberty, for revoking the laws of primogeniture and for public education.'

One does not need to minimize Paul Revere's ride in order to appreciate the greater significance of Jack Jouett's. Paul Revere was fortunate, as all New England has been fortunate, in finding a poetic historian who caught the popular imagination and wove his feat into one of the most genuine ballads of this country. Jack Jouett — the name, by the way, comes from the Huguenot de Jouetts of Touraine, France, and has been spelled in various ways — seems to have been a hearty, unaffected fellow, who stood six feet four inches and weighed two hundred and twenty pounds. He was very handsome, an excellent shot, and after the war laid aside the 'elegant sword' which had been presented to him by the Virginia Assembly, and continued to run the Old Swan Tavern.

There is nothing new in the discovery that Charlottesville is a most agreeable place in which to live. James Monroe made the discovery in 1790 and promptly moved thither, and stayed until his death in 1831. Madison, whose home was in Orange County, was always visiting here, and Lafayette loved the place. The University, of course, brings many outsiders constantly to town, and every year the charming outlying country lures a few of them to remodel an old house or to build a new one.

But for the less fortunate travelers who must return to the cold of New England or the hot winds of the West, there are a handful of readable novels which will recall to them, on quiet evenings, something of this comfortable little town in Albemarle, 'Lewis Rand,' by Mary Johnston; 'Alice of Old Vincennes,' by Maurice Thompson; 'The Crossing,' by Winston Churchill; 'Love in a Mist,' by Amélie Rives; and the 'Magnificent Adventure,' by Emerson Hough — this last dealing with the Lewis and Clark expedition.

CHAPTER V

THE UNIVERSITY OF VIRGINIA

IT is not the oldest university in the country. It is not the wealthiest nor the largest, nor does it claim the greatest number of illustrious alumni. It is, however, according to no less an authority than Stanford White, 'the most beautiful group of collegiate buildings in the world.' Its worn colonnades and exquisite ancient cornices are bathed in an atmosphere of unbroken tradition and simplicity of life unparalleled elsewhere on this continent.

You cannot see the University of Virginia from

your automobile, no matter if you slow down or even stop, although you may get one view of the famous Rotunda, modeled after the Pantheon, which Jefferson considered 'the most perfect model of spherical architecture.'

But there is no road that leads to that green Lawn that has been faced, on either side, for over a century, by ten serene pavilions with classic façades. You must leave your car and go on foot, as legend has it that Thomas Jefferson himself left his horse and walked to his own inaugural.

There are several ways of entering the grounds — all unpretentious and all lovely. Perhaps you will leave the George Rogers Clark statue behind you, pass through brick and marble gates at the east, the magnificent new Medical School on your left, and come up the Long Walk with the serpentine wall curving beside you, and the Rotunda before you gleaming through the polished magnolia leaves. Perhaps you will attempt the north side, leaving Madison Hall, with its tennis courts across the street, and, climbing the wide flight of steps, first up to Sir Moses Ezekiel's statue of Jefferson, and then on higher up to the Rotunda. Or you may drive around by the Chapel to the west, and, winding your way through alleys whose walled sides are

THE UNIVERSITY OF VIRGINIA

hung with trumpet vine and creeper, come to a halt in some quaintly paved courtyard. But however you approach, you must ultimately alight and proceed on foot, like any good pilgrim.

Argument that Jefferson himself did not design the University of Virginia flares up occasionally like the Shakespeare-Bacon controversy. It is declared, with much brandishing of documentary evidence, that Thornton and Latrobe, his two friends who designed the Capitol, are the real architects; that he derived the plan from an 'Essay on a System of National Education' by the Reverend Samuel Knox (whose proposal, by the way, is for a 'series of concentric squares facing inward with a tower in the center'); that he based his design on a plan made by the Frenchman Guennepin, which was awarded the Prix de Rome in 1805. It may also be added that Jefferson visited Marly-le-Roi in September, 1786, where he was much impressed by a famous group of buildings afterward destroyed by the Revolution — where the individual pavilions for the courtiers were arranged in two lines leading up to the casino of the king. And all agree that he was greatly influenced by Palladio; that he studied 'The Parallel of Ancient Architecture with Modern,' by Fréart de

Chambray, and that he took many notes and measurements directly from certain antique buildings he admired. It is doubtless true that Jefferson, like all normal people, was influenced by things he saw and read and heard. Perhaps he was more assimilative than the average man. But the brilliant blending of these influences into an original creation and unity is not plagiarism but genius. Any one who wishes to delve into the controversy may study his sketches, made in his own hand, and follow their gradual evolution toward this final and triumphant design. Those critics who are reluctant to admit that Jefferson was the first great American architect, as well as a statesman, a musician, a meteorologist, an author, and a scientific agriculturalist, do not remember how Nature loves to put as many eggs as possible into the basket of genius. It is not strange that a man who could design Monticello at twenty-one — a fact which has never been questioned — could, fifty years later, after a life of European contact, thus consummate his architectural ideal in the University.

But however the controversy may swing back and forth, we have before us, as we step out upon the Colonnade, the tangible vindication of a design which was unique when Jefferson proposed it, and has influenced many of the universities all over the country — from Leland Stanford, with its connecting arcades, to Columbia, with its domed library, and the Massachusetts Institute of Technology, with its colonnades.

Do not expect to be stunned by grandeur or bewildered by elaboration. Refinement of form and perfection of proportion are qualities that appeal according to the spectator's power of appreciation. Like many other supreme works of art, at first glance this one appears quite simple. Standing on the steps of the Rotunda and looking down the long lawn, we see on either side the storied porticoes of five pavilions, each to serve as an architectural example, such as the Theatre of Marcellus, the Baths of Diocletian, the Temple of Fortuna Virilis, etc. These two-storied pavilions are connected by a string of one-story rooms. A white-pillared colonnade runs in front of the whole. At one end is the Rotunda — the library. At the other is Cabell Hall — the auditorium. This is the embodiment of Jefferson's definite conviction of what a university should be — 'An academical village.' 'I consider the common plan followed in this country, but in none others, of making one large and expensive building, as unfortunately erroneous,' he wrote in 1810. 'It is infinitely better to erect a small and separate lodge for each separate professorship, with only a hall below for his class, and two chambers above for himself: joining these lodges by barracks for a certain proportion of the students, opening a covered way to give dry communication between all the schools. The whole of this arranged on an open square of grass or trees would make it, what it should be in fact, an academical village.'

This is precisely what he did. Each of those pavilions housed in the spacious corniced chambers of its upper floor the professor of one of the Schools, which all together made up the University. Virginia, by the way, was the first university in this country to open its doors as such — not growing from a college, but springing fully equipped into being, with five of its eight professors imported from Europe. Below the professor were his classrooms, and on either side of him, in small separate rooms, each with its own front door and its own fireplace, were his students. That railing along the second story connecting the pavilions marks the gallery by which the professors could communicate with one another without descending to the ground level. Behind these colonnades are a second row of one-story buildings — the Ranges. Each of these contained in the early days three hotels or refectories (in one of which, in the thirties, M. Ferron had a 'salle d'armes' and taught fencing and boxing), and constituted the entire dormitory facilities. Between the Lawn and the Ranges are alleys with clipped trees and the walled gardens of the professors. The whole plan seems amazingly simple and logical. Its faultless rhythm and symmetry defy tabulation or analysis — as in all masterpieces.

The Lawn is still the center of the University, but the temple-like pavilions are no longer exclusively possessed by the professors. With a faculty approaching the three hundred mark and a student body that has passed the two thousand, some of the pavilions have necessarily been taken over for administrative offices and classrooms. While all the old buildings remain, there are many new ones, all but two conforming in material and in architectural unity with the originals.

The visitor may wander where he will, and probably some friendly pup will elect to accompany him. For where there are boys there are dogs, and sleeping hounds lie under the circular tables in the Rotunda, and grinning bulldogs squat patiently inside and outside classroom doors, while cheerful canine vagrants attach themselves to first one group of students and then another. The dog will conduct you first to the Rotunda, with its lofty Corinthian porch and its wide balustraded esplanade, perhaps too enchanting on moonlight nights for susceptible youth.

In this beautiful edifice, inadequate now as a library, Lafayette was feasted and Edgar Allan Poe and Woodrow Wilson read. The rooms of these most famous of the University's alumni are on the West Range and marked. That of Poe — Number 13 — is now the clubroom of the Raven Society. In the Rotunda are many intimate mementoes of the founder: his Bible and Testaments, the polygraph pencil which he invented, and whose agile descendants may be seen busily working across the blackboard of great railway stations. Zolnay's bust of Poe is conspicuous on a pedestal, while other famous Virginian names, including that of Matthew Fontaine Maury, are commemorated under the dome. This is by far the most interesting building on the grounds. It was begun in the spring of 1822, and a few weeks before his death Jefferson watched the lifting of the first marble capital to the top of its pillar — the one at the southwest corner. These capitals deserve more than passing notice. After much unsatisfactory experimenting with native stone, Jefferson decided to import marble from Italy. They were shipped from Carrara in sixty-one cases weighing from three to five tons each, and were sent up the James River to the Rivanna River and received by Jefferson himself at Milton, the little village below Monticello. It was a difficult task, and caused the usual unjust criticism of extravagance.

In 1895, there was a great fire, which, more discriminating than most fires, destroyed the Public Hall, an incongruous annex which had been added to the Rotunda, and whose foundations now form the esplanade to the north. There was restoration, and expansion. The three buildings that now enclose the southern end of the Lawn were added, the grading wisely planned so that they should not detract from the dominance of the central feature — the Rotunda.

As we stroll about the grounds, we come to the McIntire open-air theater with its outdoor organ. The Law School, whose high reputation extended in the early days all over this country, and which still holds its own among the best law schools of America, overlooks the theater, as does the College Commons. The Gymnasium makes an impressive bulk to the west and the new Medical School to the east. Long before it acquired its present splendid new quarters, the Department of Medicine of the University of Virginia, as it quaintly persisted in calling itself, had won the attention of America and Europe. It has consistently turned out graduates of unusual caliber, and its roll of distinguished alumni is long and honorable. Among them are Henry Rose Carter, the father of modern quarantine, and Walter Reed, the century's greatest conqueror of disease. John Anderson, who discovered the cause of typhus fever, was a graduate of Virginia, and so was Rupert Blue, Surgeon-General of the United States Public Health Service. Dr. Blue was succeeded by another University of Virginia man, Hugh Cummings, who has been appointed to his eminent position for three terms — in itself a phenomenon. Dr. Hugh H. Young, the urologist, is another famous alumnus.

A little way out from the college grounds, topping one of the most beautiful hills in Albemarle, stands the McCormick Observatory. When Leander James McCormick presented the Observatory, fully equipped, to the University, the refracting telescope was the largest in the world. During fifty years other telescopes have superseded it in size, but not in quality. It is now the fourth largest in the country and one of the finest lenses ever made by Alvin Clark.

On another hill, more familiarly near, is the cemetery where many professors are buried, and on still another, within the grounds, is the old square house where President Monroe lived, the white-washed cottage at the end of the arcade serving as his law office. In the last Pavilion on West Lawn once lived a professor of philosophy affectionately known as 'Old Guff.' It was this Professor Mc-Guffey who compiled the school readers which are still used in countless thousands all over the country.

As we ramble up and down the cool arcades we come upon several well-placed statues. A reproduction of Houdon's Washington stands at the end of East Lawn, and Karl Bitter's Jefferson at the end of the West. In front of Cabell Hall is Sir Moses Ezekiel's Homer — which wags like to tell gullible visitors is really Uncle Remus, and that the lyre in his hand is quite an appropriate instrument.

On an elevation near the Biological Laboratory is poised a winged figure, by Gutzon Borglum, in memory of a young aviator and University of Virginia man — James R. McConnell — who died in the Great War. And intersecting and enclosing all are the serpentine walls — the unique creation of Jefferson, in which the thickness of a single brick sustains the flowing curves.

The past is vividly present in the University. Not infrequently some one says: 'I wonder what Mr. Jefferson would say to that,' as if that indefatigable man, who kept his finger on every department and activity, were only around the corner and might appear at any moment with his blue eyes clear and searching under his white hair. When the pressure of ever-increasing numbers and never sufficiently increasing funds necessitates the changing or even the abolishing of some old landmark, there is a magnificent row between radicals and conservatives.

But the present is quite as charming as the past — perhaps because there has never been a break between them. Times have changed, of course. The two hundred elegant gentlemen who had been prepared at home by English tutors and who arrived at college with their black bodyservants and saddle horses and dueling pistols have been replaced by two thousand youths from every State in the Union, many of them from local high schools. But if one will read the list of the men who fell in the Civil War — perpetuated on the bronze tablets outside the Rotunda — and compare them with the list of the men who fell in the Great War, one cannot help but be struck by the recurrence of the same substantial English names. Neither the State of Virginia nor its University has become polyglot.

Certain traditions of behavior are still as rigidly adhered to as they ever were. The honor system, which was started in 1847, is still effective to such an extent that the students guarantee the integrity of the examinations and attend to any infringement of the code themselves.

Although they no longer bring their servants with them to shine their shoes and bring in their firewood, it is the custom for Virginia students to look like gentlemen. Pressed trousers and shaven faces and clean linen are the rule, with the manners that accompany these amenities. Strangers to the University are often astonished to hear, as one group of students meets another group, no bawling out of familiarities. One low-speaking group approaches another and 'Good morning, gentlemen' is murmured as they pass.

There is, of course, a great body of idiosyncrasies here as in every venerable institution. For the University of Virginia may be so-called, in spite of the fact that it is not the most venerable in the

State. When Jefferson selected Charlottesville as
the place for his new 'academical village,' he was
roundly rated for placing it so far west. The already
firmly established College of William and Mary in
Tidewater considered Piedmont as practically on
the raw frontier of civilization. For eighty-nine
years there was no President. There was a Chair-
man of the Faculty, a Rector, and a Board of Visitors. At one time Jefferson was the Rector and
Madison and Monroe were on the Board. Dr.
Edwin Anderson Alderman assumed the first presidency in 1904, amid the usual opposition to innovation which is the birthright of all good Virginians. His conviction that a State University
should not be the privilege of an exclusive minority,
but the capstone of the public school system, was
coldly received by the dignified gentlemen of the
faculty and the hardly less dignified ones of the
student body. And even now, forced to admit the
prodigious educational strides under the régime of
President Alderman, the University still jealously
clings to certain of her original principles which dif-
ferentiated her from other American universities.
The classes are defined somewhat upon the European basis of first-year men, second-year men, etc.,
instead of Freshman, Sophomore, and the rest.

Co-education is not fully or hospitably established, although this is a State University. Only women who are over twenty years of age, and who have successfully completed two full years at some other accredited college, are admitted. And they are candidates not for cultural but only for professional and graduate degrees or for a degree from the School of Education. At present there are about a hundred women students, most of them in the School of Education, and none of them very cordially regarded by the men.

It is impossible to grasp the delicate flavor of this university in a casual stroll through the grounds. Although it is carefully studied in certain European colleges as one of the finest existing examples of architecture in the world, and although America as a whole has some vague notion of its position among the colleges of the land, Virginia itself, over-burdened with State-supported institutions, has never given it the proper financial support. Its irreplaceable beauty shines through shabbiness. The carefully trained wistaria cannot hide the crumbling cornices, nor the whitewash mend the battered columns. And not infrequently a startled student, dutifully taking notes, feels with alarm the slow collapse under him of a chair that has seen service since before the Civil War. A small corps of workmen amble here and there, patching up as best they can toppling chimneys and leaking roofs.

One solitary man — Dr. Lambeth, the superintendent of grounds and buildings — continues to plant boxwood gardens, and somehow sees to the repair of walls whose disappearance would be a loss America could never replace. Like Jefferson, he believes in the educational and spiritualizing effect of beauty. For it was the founder of the University who wrote: 'Had we built a barn for a college and log huts for accommodations, should we have had the assurance to propose to a European professor of the first order? We owed it to do, not what was to perish with ourselves, but what would remain to be respected and preserved through other ages.' It was Jefferson, too, who was the first founder of any American university which included a School of Music and Fine Arts in its original plan.

The shoe-box period of college architecture has had its evil day all over the United States, and the present generation is busy tearing down the Queen Anne structures so proudly reared by its parents and grandparents. It has recently occurred to some of the most progressive architects that a general plan of the entire college grounds should be worked out before the corner-stone is laid. Thomas Jefferson not only thought of this, but did it over a century ago, and his contribution to American architecture still stands supreme, its sun-mellowed brick clasped by green ivy, and its marble capitals silvered in the moonlight.

CHAPTER VI

MONTICELLO

MONTICELLO, three miles from the University of Virginia, is one of the most interesting houses in America. By many people it is also considered one of the most beautiful. In order to appreciate what it has stood for in the architectural history and social life of our country, one must realize that, when Jefferson started building it in 1770 (when he was twenty-one years old), it was in the inaccessible wilds of virgin country. It was necessary for him not only to conceive and draw his own plans for the house, grounds, bridle paths,

MONTICELLO, THE INTIMATE EXTENSION OF A GREAT
PERSONALITY

and gardens, but to have his own nails manufactured on the place, his wood timbered, his bricks
baked, and even to devise a cement which would
endure the damp of the underground cellars — a
formula which he himself worked out. In spite of
these enormous difficulties, this paradoxical advo-
cate of plain living made no concession in his determination to have a spacious and dignified mansion
where he could entertain in proper style the most
distinguished visitors of the world.

He was thirty years building Monticello, and
when it was completed, with its polished hardwood
floors, its conservatories, and portraits, and its
thirty-five rooms, it stood upon its mountain-top
with an air of finished elegance equal to any similar French or English country house.

We to-day, motoring over the excellent road
which leads from Charlottesville, find the three
miles very short. But look where that wagon wheel
has crossed yonder meadow and see the red clay
which even a slight pressure will cut into a deep
rut. While certain loyal sons of Albemarle insist
that they would no more think of criticizing the
gullies in their native soil than the wrinkles on their
mother's face, nevertheless it was a cruel pull in
Jefferson's day from the University up the muddy

ascent to Monticello. For the only means of transportation was the same as it had been in the time of Pharaoh. And through this clogging clay toiled the carriages which brought not only Lafayette, but the Marquis de Chastellux, the Duke de la Rochefoucauld, and countless other statesmen, soldiers, scientists, and musicians to pay their respects to the man who believed so ardently in democratic simplicity that he would not even drive to his own inauguration, but walked without an escort. Imagine their bewilderment when this beautifully built mansion, equipped with every refinement of civilization, greeted them in the midst of the backwoods!

Jefferson changed his plans for Monticello many times; he was in the public service for almost forty continuous years, and during his enforced absences the work either had to be suspended or carried on by written instructions. But he was always perfectly clear about its main features. In the first place, he chose a superb site — not a difficult thing to do in this region of incomparable hills. In the second place, he made a circular sweep of grading and planting. He had a *penchant* for spherical and octagonal lines. Although Monticello is the only private house he actually designed in en-

tirety, in nearly all the fine mansions of that period
his influence was echoed in octagon and spherical
effects. Another innovation of his is the arrangement of the servants' quarters and farm buildings.
In slavery days, and even now on many of the
old plantations, the approach to the mansion is
disfigured by the clutter of outbuildings, hen-
houses, stables, woodsheds, smokehouses, ice-
houses, and what not. Jefferson had two long low
buildings, below the level of the house and connecting with it by an underground passage. These,
divided into small separate rooms and joined by a
roofed flagged porch across the front, were servants'
quarters. What is now a gift-shop was the old
kitchen — for with plenty of pickaninnies to
scamper back and forth with covered dishes there
was no difficulty in serving hot food, even at such
a distance. It was a practical and tidy arrangement
and entirely novel. His law office and his manager's office were in small buildings in keeping
with the general architectural scheme.

The house itself is extremely interesting. The
exterior is indubitably fine and the first floor ex-
cellently suited to its primary purpose of hospitality. One passes under the lofty portico and enters into a large hall with a balcony, and opening

through double doors into the drawing-room, which overlooks the lawn. On this floor are also dining- and breakfast-rooms, two studies, two conservatories, and a few bedrooms. On the second floor are chambers and on the third a large room for billiards.

Even now, after many vicissitudes and despoiled of much of its original furnishings, there is an air of great elegance about the place. The floor of the drawing-room was cut and fitted by hand, native hard woods being used. The darker centers of each of the highly polished squares are cherry, the lighter borders beech, and after more than a century of use they show no sign of wear.

A peculiarity of the hall is the absence of stairs. Jefferson did not consider these necessities as architectural features to be emphasized, and in all of his buildings he was inclined to tuck them away as inconspicuously as possible. It is said that he objected to the tendency of lingering groups to block the stairway at parties, and determined to avoid this in his own house. Whatever the reason, in each of the two narrow passages which lead off at right angles from the central hall are narrow winding staircases barely two feet wide. Those that lead down to the basement are only thirty-one inches wide. His treatment of sleeping arrangements was equally curious. There were no bedsteads in the chambers, the beds being built into alcoves in the thick walls, and in one room linen closets are placed above. Between his own chamber and study is a connecting space five feet by six. In this was fitted a bed that could be drawn up to the ceiling during the day, giving free passage between the rooms. From this study an enclosed stair leads to an upper room where at times a guard was stationed. Three oval openings in the upper wall are said to have been filled by portraits, removed by a late owner. But they could have served as peek-holes for the guard.

Jefferson had such a tremendous range of political and educational interests that many people do not realize that he had also one of those fertile minds which delight in working out ingenious mechanical contrivances. The man, who, while being twice President of the United States, Minister to France, and Governor of Virginia, found time to write over thirty thousand letters, was also the inventor of the mould-board plough — a great improvement over the primitive straight or coulter plough. He invented the patent self-closing buggy-top, the revolving swivel-chair (the original of which stands in his study), and the polygraph pencil. He took great satisfaction in carrying to church a cane that he devised which unfolded into a chair. Monticello is packed with evidences of his ingenuity. The clock over the front door, with the weights arranged to hang down in the corners out of sight, is one example. Others are the folding ladder, the weather vane on the portico roof connecting with the compass on the ceiling, the dumbwaiter concealed in the dining-room mantel and connecting with the locked wine-vault below, and the folding doors between the hall and the drawing-room, so arranged that when one is closed the other shuts mechanically — a familiar device to us now, from its use on many trolley cars.

However, it is none of these details, fascinating as they are, which give Monticello its atmosphere and its distinction. It is famous because it is the intimate extension of a great personality, and was for so long the fitting background for a brilliant social and domestic life. Jefferson's wife, Martha Wayles, who was the handsome young widow of Bathurst Skelton, lived at Monticello only ten years, leaving at her death two little daughters. It was Martha, the elder, who was educated in France while her father was Minister there, and who later married Thomas Mann Randolph, Governor of Virginia. She was during Jefferson's life the mistress of Monticello. And during these years the spacious house was a continual center of hospitality. Besides all the formal entertaining of visitors from Europe and all parts of the United States, cousins and grandchildren, nieces and nephews and kin of the most nebulous connection came to Monticello for visits lasting for months and even for years. Jefferson was demonstrative and tender in all his personal relationships, and it did not disturb him in the least when the old steward complained that he would 'cut up a fine beef and two days later it was gone.' This does not imply that the menu was a simple one. Jefferson had a taste for French cookery, and the elaborate table at Monticello caused Patrick Henry to shout, in one of his denunciations of the great man, 'He hath abjured his native victuals.'

The sleeping arrangements were on as generous a scale as the culinary. It was said that Mrs. Randolph had put up as many as fifty guests overnight.

It is not hard to re-vision some of these scenes, which have been told and pictured so often that they have become part of the vibration of the place. We can picture the blinding snowstorm through which Jefferson and his bride came riding double on a horse in the middle of the night, their chaise having broken down. Monticello was not yet finished, and they spent the night in the small cottage which was afterwards used as his office, and is still called 'Honeymoon Lodge.' Legend has it that, in order to keep warm, Jefferson played his fiddle and Mrs. Jefferson danced. However, in Virginia then, as now, there were speedier ways to get warm, and we have no reason to think that a hot toddy was scorned by the two chilled young people. We can picture the June morning when Jack Jouett came galloping up the hill to warn the Governor of the State of the approach of Tarleton and his men. We recall the hasty departure, first, of the family and of Jefferson himself, and immediately after, the sudden swarming of Tarleton's troops over the grounds and house. Although the negro slaves were quick-witted enough to hide many of the valuables under the floor of the front portico, there was no damage done. 'Tarleton behaved very genteelly with me,' Jefferson said afterwards. Again we can picture the great enthusiast for enlightenment, whose ambitious schemes for general education included district grammar and classical schools, a free library and college for every State in the Union, standing on the roof of the side passage, his eye fixed to a telescope, following with intentness the slow erection of the distant University. We can see him, an old man, playing on his violin in the sunshine of the conservatory, still insisting on holding the instrument under his chin in what his critics declared to be 'the effeminate European manner,' instead of against his stomach in the sturdy American fashion.

And finally we can imagine him, at the end of his strenuous life, leaning back in the chair that still stands in his study, one frail old hand raised as he made his slaves into freemen.

Jefferson died poor — which is not to be wondered at — and Mrs. Randolph, an elderly woman, had to leave the home of her girlhood and the scene of her busy and happy cares.

In 1830, James Barclay bought the place, and six years later sold it to Commodore Uriah P. Levy, of New York, for twenty-seven hundred dollars. At his death, Commodore Levy left it to the people of the United States, with the provision that if Congress failed to take ownership, it should go successively to the State of Virginia and the Portuguese-Hebrew Congregation of New York. The courts decided that these trusts were too vague, and prolonged litigation among the heirs followed. The case was finally decided in favor of the Commodore's nephew, Jefferson M. Levy of New York, who fortunately had the means and the patriotism to restore the house and grounds, both of which had fallen into greatest disrepair. In 1923 the Thomas Jefferson Memorial Foundation came into being, and purchased grounds and mansion for $500,000, to keep it as a national shrine. The trees which Jefferson planted have been surgically treated, the grounds put in repair, and gradually the original furniture is being collected again. It is open to the public daily for a small fee.

Visitors to this historic home stop on their way up at the cemetery in the woods where Jefferson, his family, and some of his closest friends are buried. It would be better if they could stop on the way down, for after an hour at Monticello even the most superficial visitor must have caught some idea of the versatile tastes and amazing mental and physical vitality of the man who built it and who dispensed from it such affectionate personal friendship and such magnificent hospitality.

With characteristic incisiveness he wrote the inscription for the plain shaft that marks the enclosure, within which he is buried. It reads:

Here was buried
Thomas Jefferson
Author of the Declaration of
Independence, of the Statute
of Virginia for Religious
Freedom, and Father of the
University of Virginia.

There is no mention, you notice, of his having been twice President of the United States and Minister to France and Governor of Virginia. Those honors he felt had been bestowed upon him. The other titles he had won through his own definite effort. The obelisk we see to-day is not the original, which was so hacked and mutilated by curiosity seekers, that it was finally removed. The scarred shaft stands on the campus of the University of Missouri. The monument in the Monticello Cemetery is twice the size of the one which Jefferson designed, and whose measurements he specified.

Jefferson died on July 4, 1826, fifty years to a day from the signing of the Declaration of Independence of which he was the author, and a few hours earlier than John Adams, also an ex-President, died in Quincy, Massachusetts.

CHAPTER VII

SHORT DRIVES AROUND ALBEMARLE

WHILE it is still characteristic of Virginia that the social and political life goes by counties — of which there are a round hundred — rather than by towns and villages, it was even more definitely so when the original divisions were made. In each county a few important plantation-owners, secure upon their extensive acres, decided public questions, set the standard of culture, and entertained the traveler. The tourist from other parts of the country cannot help noticing that there still exist in this State scattering and unconnected settlements, with the large plantation houses set far back from the road — many of them completely hidden. The thrifty New England village with its well-kept green, the ambitious small city of the West — one does not see them here. The owners of the comfortable estates like to call themselves farmers, but they have small resemblance to the gallused and calloused sons of toil of Maine or Iowa. They correspond more closely to the English country squire.

Albemarle was set apart from Goochland County in 1745. It was named for William Anne Keppel, second Earl of Albemarle, who was Governor-in-Chief of Virginia from 1735 to 1754. We have no record that this busy nobleman ever visited America, or that it ever entered his head that his musical title would echo for so many years to come in remote Virginia.

One of the earliest, the most typical, and the most historically interesting of the plantations in Albemarle was Shadwell, the home of Colonel Peter Jefferson, and the birthplace of his son Thomas. Colonel Jefferson had received a patent of a thousand acres, named it after the parish in London where his wife was born, and later procured an additional four hundred acres on the east from his friend William Randolph; the agreeable price of this acquisition being 'Henry Weatherbourne's biggest bowl of Arrack punch.'

It is only a five-mile drive from Charlottesville to Shadwell, and although the original farmhouse of a story and a half with its huge chimneys was destroyed by fire a hundred and fifty years ago, the site remains, marked by the sycamores which Thomas Jefferson planted there on his twenty-first birthday. It is a lovely place, with an extended panorama which without doubt influenced Jefferson's invariable selection of building sites with fine views. The visitor to Shadwell will notice that the painted wooden marker by the roadside says that Thomas Jefferson, third President of the United States, was born here April 2, 1743. But in the iron grill farther up the hill the granite slab which marks the exact site of the house states that Jefferson was born here April 13, 1743. This discrepancy of dates is neither a mistake nor an obstetrical phenomenon, but is due to the change from the Old Style Calendar to the New Style, which took place at this time.

Colonel Jefferson was a man of enormous stature and enormous strength: he was a distinguished surveyor and politically important in the county. His son came naturally by his love of hospitality, for Shadwell was for years the stopping-place of all passers-by, even the Indian chiefs on their way to and from the Capital. When it was burned down in 1770, Monticello was sufficiently completed for Jefferson's family to move in.

It is not only Shadwell and Monticello which speak of Jefferson. This whole section of Albemarle is associated with him. On our way back from the birthplace the road runs directly across Pantops, one of his favorite farms. It is worth a détour to circle around through this exalted orchard and see the superb view and to realize that Jefferson so loved this place that when he was President of the United States he found time to design the chicken coops for it. We read that he would not permit his granddaughter to build a henhouse on Pantops until the following summer when he would be there and have time to supervise in design and location. Pantops was at one time a boys' school; and is now private property, and whoever loves columbine in the spring and wild iris will find whole sheets of them upon the wooded slopes of Pantops Orchard. Shadwell village used to be of some importance. There was even a large carding factory with a hundred operatives, sawmills and stores, and, as the river was then navigable to this point, there was much shipping, in flat-bottomed boats, of tobacco packed in hogsheads. There were tobacco warehouses and river trade at Milton, too. But now the chief interest about this little place is that it was here that Jefferson received the capitals of the Rotunda.

There are few men who have left such impress upon the architecture and landscape of their native heath. Three miles from the gates of the University up the Ivy Road is a small station called Woods. A quarter of a mile to the right of this stands Farmington, one of the famous estates of the county, now being remodeled into a club house. For it, as for many of the fine houses of that period, Jefferson's suggestion was sought. The large octagonal structure in front of the old-fashioned square main building suggests him: so do the circular upper windows, and the full-height hall behind a Doric portico which has caught the Jeffersonian proportion if even it lacks the Jeffersonian detail. Here, too, are hidden passages, leading through tunnels below grade, under colonnades and arcades above grade, past doors of the servants' quarters, behind an area wall supported by flying buttresses to the stable three hundred feet away. In spite of this provision for the servants and outbuildings, the usual clutter of sheds grew up and obscured the beauty of Farmington, and for years the black-and-white marble floor of the portico was shabby and an air of gentle disrepair hung over everything. But nothing could dim the ineffable radiance of the wide view from the side porch, comprising seven counties, or lessen the dignity of the dark yew tree in front. Farmington is now being restored, its grounds and trees repaired. The house will be remodeled for its new uses, and in its semi-public character will give many outsiders an opportunity to study and enjoy it.

On our way back to Charlottesville we can make a short détour of half a mile from Ivy Depot to Locust Hill. Here, in a house which overlooked the tranquil rolling pastures, was born, in 1774, Meriwether Lewis. A bronze plaque on a granite boulder marks the place, and probably the same soft sunshine lay upon the same luminous meadows then as now. At eight, little Meriwether Lewis was an intrepid hunter: at eighteen, he assumed the management of Locust Hill. As usual in country districts there are many legends about him as a youth, and about his remarkable mother, who, when she was nearly eighty, rode eight miles on horseback to visit the sick, among whom she had a great reputation for her cures.

If one follows the Ivy Road for two miles past the University just before it runs under the railroad bridge, there is a branch to the right — the Garth Road — which winds for a dozen miles through charming upland country and again to Ivy. It passes isolated places where the stables are much larger than the residences, and the paddocks more conspicuous than the gardens, for this is the region where thoroughbred race-horses are raised, and on every side their slim outlines are silhouetted against the sky. If one has courage to penetrate a certain rutted turn to the right, about six miles along, it will bring him out into a singularly remote and rolling stretch of open land still called 'The Barracks.' Here, during Revolutionary times, four thousand of King George's Hessians were sent by Congress as prisoners of war, while their superior officers sought quarters among the neighboring gentry. There is nothing left of the dormitories and gardens, the theater, coffee-house, and bathhouse that Lossing tells us that these aliens constructed at The Barracks. But in the Ragged Mountains are many descendants of the deserters, their features, names, and natures still noticeably Hessian.

Another pleasant drive from Charlottesville is the seventeen smoothly paved miles to Scottsville,

originally called Scotts Ferry, and at that time the
most important settlement in the county. The
smooth water of the James and the sheltering hill
gave it natural advantages, and here the usual
cheerful Colonial appurtenances of courthouse,
prison stocks, and pillory were erected. Where they
stood may still be traced about a mile west of the
town on the estate of Valmont. It is said that the
tenant house is the Old Courthouse, which was
partly demolished and rebuilt with the original
timbers a few years after the Revolutionary War.
A hundred years ago, Scotts Ferry was an extremely
active trading center. As many as a hundred large
valley wagons could unload in a day their flour,
bacon, venison, butter, cheese, and beeswax. Here
the majority of students for the University arrived
by boat. But perhaps the most significant departure from Scotts Ferry was that of the first Mc-
Cormick reapers. This incalculably precious invention, which Secretary Seward declared had pushed
civilization westward thirty miles a year, which
was destined to do the work of twelve million men
and to abolish our agricultural peasantry so effectively that we have had to import our muscle from
foreign countries ever since, was the result of years
of experimenting first by Robert McCormick and

then by his sons. To get the first seven reapers to
the West, they had to be carried in wagons from
the shop where they had been made in Rockbridge
County to Scottsville. Thence they traveled by
canal to Richmond, were reshipped down the James
River to the Atlantic Ocean, and around Florida
to New Orleans, were transferred here to a river
boat that went up the Mississippi and Ohio Rivers
to Cincinnati, and from Cincinnati were shipped
again by wagon to their various points of destination. And even with all this expense of cartage, the
reapers paid for themselves the first year.

The most romantic sight in Albemarle is without
question the ruins of the old Barbour mansion at
Barboursville. When the great, beautiful house
was destroyed by fire on a long-ago Christmas Day,
the rubbish was removed, but the lofty pillars of
the portico and the exquisitely laid brick walls were
left standing. Now ivy half conceals these crumbling outlines: periwinkle weaves a mat of green and
blue about their base. Great trees are growing
in the drawing-room, for the roof is the blue Virginia sky. Antique box hedges frame the lawn and
the old walks and gardens are still there. Although
less extensive, the place is as beautiful as Kenil-
worth. Ruskin, who declared that no house had

fulfilled its highest mission until it had become a ruin, would be entirely satisfied with the Barbour place.

The Nine-Mile Circuit is another popular drive, starting out Rugby Road, the fashionable suburban district, passing the Fair Grounds, swinging into pretty country, passing the birthplace site of William Wirt, three times Attorney-General of the United States, and entering Charlottesville again by Park Street, the old residential section of the town.

Two hours will take one through the rolling and red-splashed Greenwood country, to the Miller School and back again — one of the most admirable schools in Virginia. Samuel Miller was the son of a remarkable mother and of an English lawyer who did not give his name to his children. The young mother was a weaver, and she gathered her wool from the briars where the sheep had grazed. With the money she earned by this pitiful labor, she paid the tuition of her two boys in the best school in the vicinity. On winter mornings she could be seen whipping the barefooted lads down the mountain to school. They both grew into unusual men. John left his younger brother an estate of one hundred thousand dollars, and when Samuel died in 1869 he left about a million dollars to establish and maintain the Miller Manual Labor School of Albemarle. This was not only one of the first schools in America to emphasize industrial education, but it was an extraordinary enterprise in a Southern community, where manual labor has never been considered as dignified. It opened in 1878 with twenty-one boys. The first girls were admitted in 1884. Now it has a hundred pupils, twelve hundred acres of land, and a dozen buildings of good design and adequate equipment. The higher courses correspond to the academic grades of a modern high school with additional instruction in woodwork, metalwork, foundry work, mechanics, agriculture, etc. Jennie Miller's determination for two small barefooted boys has fulfilled itself in the lives of hundreds of penniless Albemarle children.

Throughout the county of Albemarle everywhere are pleasant estates of local fame and of family legend, and lucky the traveler who has a letter of introduction to one of them. Otherwise he will only catch a glimpse of the boxwood hedges of Donegal, or of the yew trees which were brought from England for Tallwood, no one remembers how long ago. The plans of Morven are said to have been furnished by Jefferson, who also ordered from Paris

PLEASANT ESTATES OF LOCAL FAME AND OF FAMILY
LEGEND

the mantel of Carrara marble for its drawing-room.
The same honor is claimed for Redlands, built by
Robert Carter in 1789, and for Estouteville on its
high plateau. Castalia and Cloverfields still maintain their traditions and hospitalities, and many are
their memories of hunt breakfasts, balls, and garden parties. And not only memories of the past but
the gay anticipation of the morrow, for the love
of a good time is a perennial part of the Virginian
disposition, and somehow there is always time
and equipment for a party. Cobham, Castle Hill,
Belvoir, Music Hall, Enniscorthy, Dunlora, Bremo,
and Edgehill — the stranger cannot hope to see
more than their chimney tops and perhaps not
even that much. To him the names can only be
musical syllables.

But for those whom friendly fortune has placed
in Albemarle, these old places are associated with
a hundred adventures, humorous and romantic:
with

'open jasmine-muffled lattices,
And groups under the dreaming garden trees
And the full moon, and the white evening star...'

CHAPTER VIII

FOLLOWING THE SPOTSWOOD TRAIL

THE visitor to Charlottesville who is fortunate enough to have a fine day upon his hands can hardly do better than to swing around in the same bright circle of eighty miles which was first discovered two hundred-odd years ago by the Knights of the Golden Horseshoe. This trip, with the happy legend about it is one of the prettiest in Virginia. It runs in this wise:

Alexander Spotswood had been sent over from England to be Governor of Virginia. He was young and handsome, with a soldierly record behind him, with executive ability and a delightful sense of gayety. He was practical enough, as the iron furnaces he established at Germanna testify. But he was also susceptible to romance and vivacious display. It is he who is credited with sailing up the Rappahannock on a boat made musical with English skylarks, which he released in the meadows just below the falls in Spottsylvania. Children on their way to school in Fredericksburg still insist that they can hear these larks singing in the early morning. But as youth becomes maturity, something seems to happen to their ears, for only common meadowlarks are heard by grown-ups.

Spotswood is credited with having cordially urged the Indians to send their children to William and Mary College. He was also the chief and victorious participant in the gorgeously spectacular fight with Blackbeard the Pirate, whose head was subsequently brought home on a pikestaff. These and a dozen other picturesque stories cling to the name of the spirited young governor.

At this time — 1714 — nothing was known of the country on the other side of the mountains. Although the Jesuits and a few adventurers were supposed to have crossed the range, Orange County extended, as far as Virginians were concerned, to the Pacific Ocean, and people agreed that the Mississippi River rose in the Blue Ridge. It occurred to Alexander Spotswood that it would be fun to explore a bit. He thereupon invited any of the neighboring planters who felt so inclined to come along with him, and promptly a party assembled that looked and acted far more like a picnic than a serious expedition. John Fontaine, an ensign of the British army, was a member of the party and his journal gives us all the details. 'The trumpets sounded to horse and we were away,' he writes. 'Lord Spotswood was dressed in a green velvet riding-suit with high boots of soft Russian leather and plumed hat.' Besides the leader and his peers were mules and pack-saddles and servants. There was Virginia red wine and white wine, Irish usquebaugh, brandy, shrub, two sorts of rum, champagne, canary, cherry punch, cider, and after all that, 'etc.'

It was a fine August morning, and the whole crowd was about to set off when some one remembered that it would be necessary to shoe the horses if they were to climb mountains. The roads of lower Virginia were so soft and sandy that this necessity had not arisen before. And so with much chaffing, every one had to dismount, and there was quite a delay while horseshoes were made and fitted — an incident which later suggested the name of the band. Finally, however, the horses were all shod and they again started out, joined along the way by various additional sporting members of the Colony. They came to Germanna, on the edge of the Spottsylvania wilderness, where the Governor had built a summer house for himself. They stayed here awhile and then proceeded west. The weather was cloudless. They shot deer and elk. There was much jollity and no mishaps. When the cavalcade finally crossed the Blue Ridge and saw the valley of the Shenandoah far below, they had a magnificent celebration. 'We drank the King's health in champagne and fired a volley,' John Fontaine writes; 'the Princess' health in Burgundy and fired a volley: and all the rest of the Royal Family's health in claret and fired a volley. We drank the Governor's health in rum punch and fired a volley. We called the highest mountain Mount George and the one we crossed over Mount Spotswood.'

Having thus reached their agreeable destination, they turned around and came clattering home, having taken three weeks to cover the ground which we fly over in half a day. (We may, if we wish to extend our drive to a full day, continue on to Elkton and Harrisonburg and thence back to Charlottesville via Staunton.)

It is not recorded that this ascent of the Blue Ridge was of great pioneering value. But it so caught the fancy of the participants that they decided to commemorate it and themselves by establishing an Order of Knighthood. Remembering the incident of the horseshoeing, Governor Spotswood named them 'Sir Knights of the Golden Horseshoe' and sent to England for a number of small golden horseshoes engraved with the words: 'Sic juvat transcendere montes.' (Thus we swear to cross the mountains.) The King made the Governor Sir Alexander Spotswood, but he neglected to pay for the horseshoes. So the newly made baronet paid for them out of his own pocket. And he furthermore liberally declared that 'any gentleman was entitled to wear the golden horseshoe who could prove that he had drank to His Majesty's health on Mount George.'

It is this Spotswood Trail that can be followed to-day over excellent roads through isolated small villages, up and down steep gorges, beside tumbling mountain rivulets, through forests flushed in the spring with redbud, and white with the level

THE SPOTSWOOD TRAIL THROUGH ISOLATED SMALL
VILLAGES

branches of dogwood — up and up to the top of the mountains.

The stone pyramid, with its inset tablet bearing the names of the Spotswood party, is not placed so as to command the most effective view. One should go a mile farther, to where the mountains roll back on either side. From here the Shenandoah Valley stretches out far below in ineffable beauty. It is one of the most splendid panoramas in Virginia, and one doubts if there is a man with soul so dead that, when he sees it, he would not toss his plumed hat into the air, if he had a plumed hat, and drink champagne to the King's health, if he had champagne.

Good and well-marked as the roads are which circle in from Charlottesville, from Orange and from Harrisonburg, the country through which they pass is singularly unkempt. There are lumber camps here and there, brutally despoiling the wooded slopes, but except for occasional small hamlets, there is practically no other sign of activity. Here and there a field has been ploughed for wheat or corn, but there are no gardens, only a few poor cattle and sheep — no poultry. Only the opulence of the golden sunshine redeems from squalor the tumbledown cabins of the black people and the forlorn houses of the white.

Yet the sunbonneted women who look up to smile at the passing automobile, the children who wave delighted hands, and the tall men who incline their heads with grave friendliness as they pass on horseback, are by no means inferior in physique or carriage. They are fair-skinned, blue-eyed, and yellow-haired, with the peculiar dignity of the Anglo-Saxon. Should you stop to talk with them, you would find them entirely free from subservience. If you should study below the dirt-coarsened skin, you would detect a fine facial outline, well-modeled skull, and hands and feet by no means plebeian. Should you stay longer, you would detect, as you joined them in their meals of fat meat, 'snaps,' and corncakes, words and phrases that were in good usage in Elizabethan times. And at night, lying on your mattress of corn shucks under the tin roof, there would come tinkling up to you snatches of ballads that might have been heard by Spenser.

Any one of these ignorant and isolated families, forlornly held in a back pocket of the mountains, is typical of thousands, for seventy-five per cent of Virginia's population live outside the cities, even outside the towns. The great lovely estates account for only a handful. Many more must be numbered among these mountaineers, whose habits of speech and physical characteristics have persisted for three centuries. Here is undiluted Virginia stock, which means undiluted English stock: not the England of to-day, but the robust and Rabelaisian, the sentimental and belligerent England of Elizabeth. The mountain barriers have kept their speech primitive and their bones straight, but have limited their mentality and distorted their emotions into suspicions and hatreds.

It is obvious that this scattering nature of settlement in Virginia has retarded the development of the public school system. Any one who is used to the frequent and well-equipped public school buildings throughout New England and the West must consider the situation in this State from several different angles. Although the constitution of the Commonwealth of Virginia contains the clause, 'The General Assembly shall establish and maintain an efficient system of free schools throughout the State,' the situation has never been, and is not now a simple one.

In the first place, Virginia was not founded upon democratic, but upon aristocratic principles. This extended to all of its institutions and customs and became part of the fiber of its social consciousness. The wealthy planters assumed that education was a function of the home and individual responsibility. When public schools were attempted, the poorer settlers, who were just as proud as their financial superiors, resented the proffered aid as pauperization. Every one rather inclined to agree with the Governor, who remarked, 'I thank God there are no free schools in Virginia.'

Jefferson's proposed plan of public education in 1779 was doomed to failure. It was based upon his political philosophy of local self-government, and those in authority represented the aristocratic element, which did not see the necessity of taxing itself to establish institutions which it did not personally patronize. This ingrained prejudice against free schooling, held by rich and poor alike, thwarted the various attempts to establish public education. The Civil War put an effective end to any progress which had been made. When Virginia at last came to realize the necessity for reconstructing her social and educational ideals, she found herself confronted by the several very acute handicaps which still exist. As we said before, seventy-five per cent of her population live not only away from the city, but away from any center whatever. This is the first difficulty. The second is the necessity for a dual system of schools — white and colored. The third difficulty has been in working out any equalization of educational opportunity. Many counties which contain a large percentage of children of school age possess almost nothing in the way of taxable property. A great effort is being made to enlarge the State appropriation and to use it so as to equalize the varying local support which the various counties are able to give. There has never been any problem among the well-to-do, who still either establish small private schools or engage tutors for their children until they are old enough to be sent to preparatory school and college. But the middle class — which is the foundation of culture in all social structure — has been ignored. The instinctive mannerliness and graceful demeanor which is part of the inheritance and training of all Virginians has obscured their lack of substantial and genuine education. Now these defects are being recognized, and being faced squarely and intelligently. During the last decade a more enlightened point of view has evolved both in legislator and mountaineer. More and better schools are being built. Higher salaries are offered to teachers, the standards of scholarship have been raised, technical training has been dignified, and political influence lessened. The colored schools are sharing in this constructive programme. In the cities they compare favorably with the white schools. Perhaps the less said about them in rural districts the better. While it is true that this dual system of schools is a great burden to the State, Virginia is fortunate in being entirely free from the hordes of foreign-born children who so impede educational progress in the North.

The recognition of her peculiar problems was Virginia's first step in meeting them. After that, good roads have come as saviors to the distant regions. Now free buses carry the children to and from school, and the State is assuming a juster share of the financial responsibility too long confined to each separate county.

With the good roads have come another development, perhaps not wholly inconsistent when we recall Governor Spotswood's array of liquid refreshment. Certain isolated sections in the Virginian mountains have long been dedicated to the mystic distillation of 'moonshine.' Those labyrinthine paths which wind perplexingly up and into the mountains lead to fastnesses unassailable because undiscoverable. There, in secret retreats, the mountaineer, who used to concoct only enough of that potent liquor to lull himself into pleasant dreams, is busier than he has ever been before in his life. And he, too, is making use of the good roads to dispose of his magic white water.

Thus, by one of those paradoxes of fortune, the once penniless moonshiner finds it possible to send his sons and daughters even farther than the public schools. Their road goes beyond the route of the public school bus. In shining automobiles, these fair-haired, soft-voiced boys and girls are pouring out into the great world, and finding their places in the colleges and universities thereof.

CHAPTER IX

LYNCHBURG AND TOBACCO

WHILE the political and social life of Virginia is meticulously regulated by its hundred counties, the three major geographical distinctions are defined with equal clarity. These three great divisions are Tidewater along the coastal plain, the Piedmont Plateau running through the central section of the State, and the Appalachian Mountain Province, which includes the Blue Ridge and the Great Valley.

A most varied and lovely stretch of Piedmont is

THE CANAL, LYNCHBURG

spanned by the ninety-mile drive between Charlottesville and Lynchburg, which latter city is
solidly built up and down the sharp sides of a
cluster of hills with the James River at their base.

Lynchburg obviously obtained its industrial
importance through its temperate climate and its
advantageous location. It obtained its name in the
following way: A little over two centuries ago,
a fifteen-year-old Irish lad, nursing a grievance
against his stepmother, decided to run away from
home and 'go to America.' But when the boat on
which he had begged passage began to put out to
sea, he was frightened, and jumped overboard and
began to swim back toward the green hills of Ireland. He was, however, promptly rescued in spite
of himself, dumped on deck, and the ship proceeded.
And in due time the unwilling adventurer found
himself in Virginia, and apprenticed to a wealthy
tobacco planter in what is now Louisa County.

In those spacious days amazing opportunities
were open even to as unheroic a person as little
Charles Lynch. He grew up, married the daughter
of the planter, moved to Chestnut Hill on the
James River, about a mile from the present site of
Lynchburg, acquired large royal grants of land and
six children. It was one of these children, John

Lynch, who later conceived the idea of establishing a ferry across the river, and then of establishing a town on the hill over which the ferry road went. This, in 1787, was the beginning of Lynchburg.

The Lynches left their mark as well as their name upon the spot where they chose to live. The daughter of the planter whom the first Charles Lynch married was a devout Quaker, and, although she was disowned for marrying outside of the Church, she was afterward reinstated and brought her husband with her. It was she who was responsible for the establishing of the Quakers in Lynchburg — that peculiarly admirable sect which has been without exception an asset to every community of their adoption. The first Quakers in Lynchburg met in a log meeting-house which was burned down, as was the frame one which followed it. In 1791, a stone meeting-house was built near the same site as the two earlier ones, and this was the center for many years of the social and religious life of the town. It was also the focal point of much fighting during the Civil War, and Northern soldiers as well as Southern were buried in its graveyard. It is this old stone meeting-house that the Presbyterians restored twenty-five years ago, using the original corner-stone and calling it the Quaker Memorial

Presbyterian Church. The most historical landmark in the modern city, it manages, despite its
combination name, to retain much of that exquisite
austerity characteristic of those disturbingly logical
Christians who have always been quite willing to
die for peace, not by fighting for it, but by refusing
to fight. Warmed by the mild winter sunshine, or
under the drifting leaves of autumn or the verdure
of summer, the modest headstones slant heavily to
the earth. Many of the names are obliterated —
forgotten as completely as the serene faces of the
men in broad-brimmed hats and women in coal-
scuttle bonnets who sat quietly along the plain
wooden benches. But the individual names are not
of so much importance. Wherever the Quakers
have lived they have woven a staunch thread into
the civic and religious fiber of the community,
which is their best perpetuity.

Before we leave the Lynch family, we must recall
that it was Charles, one of the six children of the
runaway Irish lad, who is responsible for 'Lynch
Law.' It is a mistake, however, to think that this
practice originally had anything in common with
stringing offenders up on telegraph poles or crooked
apple trees. It was started after sober deliberation
as a necessary protective measure against certain

bands of Tory desperadoes who were making a great deal of trouble. The State could not or did not afford adequate protection against these bandits. It remained for Colonel Charles Lynch to organize a band of men to pursue the marauders and capture them. Some were flogged, some were imprisoned. Only a negligible number were ever executed. The fact that Lynch Law was sanctioned by the General Assembly in 1782 shows that its nature was orderly at that time.

Northerners, who think that tea precipitated the Revolution, may be surprised to learn that Southerners give that place of honor to tobacco. The irritating duties and regulations which England imposed upon its cultivation led to some tobacco riots, which led to certain executions for treason, which led to a considerable diminution of Virginia loyalty to the Mother Country. And at this juncture the connection between the Church and tobacco became vital. The clergy received their salaries in tobacco, and naturally did not favor any agitation which would affect its production. 'The Establishment is indeed Tobacco,' wrote the Reverend Hugh Jones in his pamphlet in 1724 — a statement which was considerably confusing to the gentlemen in London who controlled the plantations with the detachment peculiar to absentee landlords. Moncure Conway has entertainingly described the situation in his 'Tobacconalia.'

'Early in the eighteenth century Tobacco had become the currency of the colony. By the law of 1696 the salary of every clergyman had been fixed at sixteen thousand pounds of tobacco per annum. But the value of such a salary was variable, by reason of changes in the market price, consequent on the quantity shipped to Europe and also on account of the quality of the tobacco. In some parishes only "Orinoco" could be raised, which was inferior to "sweet-scented." Many a poor clergyman's household was filled with joy at the tidings of his promotion from an "Orinoco" Parish to a "sweet-scented" parish, as they are described in the old books. The parishes where no tobacco could be raised were frankly left without ministration of the Established Church. Here came Baptists, and Quakers, and peripatetic ranters or any rabid separatist who drifted past. The wandering "parsons" connected with the Establishment were often illiterate, there being no American episcopate, and ministers having to go in person to England for ordination. . . .

'The sweet-scented parsons were very insistent

upon a correct counting of plants by the vestryman, and showed a pious anxiety to prevent de-
terioration of the tobacco crop, or of its price
to the injury of Christ's Kingdom in Virginia.
During the drought of 1755, when the people could
not pay their tobacco debts in kind, the only credi-
tors who demanded such payment were some of the
clergy.

'This was the beginning of many lawsuits, culminating in "The Parsons Case," which was the first
heard before Colonel John Henry, father of Patrick,
as magistrate. Patrick's uncle, for whom the orator
was named, was one of the petitioners of the act.
He flamed out with such an arraignment of the
clergy for grinding the suffering people that he
broke their authority and became the darling of the
Presbyterians and other dissenters. His arraignment of the King was the virtual settlement of the
case of the Colonies versus the King. When the
Stamp Act presently came, Patrick Henry held
the people of Virginia in his hand.'

Virginia now ranks third in the tobacco-produc-
ing States of the Union, its annual output amount-
ing to about $144,000,000. Lynchburg, whose first
little tobacco warehouse was built in 1786, has a
daily handling capacity of 250,000 pounds, a great

portion of it being bought for export to foreign countries. It is the dark tobacco center, as Danville is the bright tobacco center of this enormous industry.

It is possible to start for Lynchburg from Charlottesville along a picturesque but difficult back way, where high red-clay banks open to reveal long stretches of woodland and pasture, and an occasional small stone church or mill. After a rain, one may have to ford streams, and if it happens to be Sunday he will pass men and women going to church on horseback. One may jog along here for half a day and never meet an automobile. Faint footsteps meander off into hills to cabins whose solitude is incredible to the city dweller.

But as few tourists will take the time to plough up and down hill between the red-clay banks of the Old Lynchburg Road, so even fewer will care to approach the modern city through the long chronicle of history. It has its historical memories and landmarks, and plenty of them. The fort where General Jubal Early repulsed the Yankees is always carefully pointed out to all Northern visitors. In its early days the city was busy organizing churches and schools and newspapers. It had its excitements over wet and dry elections, duels and public executions. It had floods and fires, even an earthquake and a period of falling stars. It boasted distinguished visitors and famous residents. Mark Twain's parents stayed here long enough for him to get a Langhorne incorporated into his name. Nancy Hanks lived near by, and Poplar Forest, the summer home which Jefferson built so that he could get away from the too insistent press of people at Monticello, and where he composed his series of 'Notes on Virginia,' is still used as a residence and a delightful one. But unlike many Southern cities, Lynchburg's primary interest is not in the past, but in the present.

The numerous manufactories employ about seven thousand workers, who seem quite contented with no labor unions, no agitators, and a conspicuously low rate of turnover. Its stable and homogeneous population of forty thousand support a commission form of government. Lynchburg, rich and enlightened, is not tributary to anything — not even to its long and honorable past.

And yet, as we poke the nose of our car down one of those dizzying streets that lead abruptly to the splendid modern bridge, for a moment we are conscious of the span between the present and the past. For we are passing over a river which has

been an important factor in the development of an
important city, and which a hundred years ago was
the main thoroughfare between here and Richmond. In that era fleets of bateaux plied constantly
back and forth, taking a week to go and ten days to
return. These bateaux were forty or fifty feet long,
about two feet deep, and from four to five feet wide.
Each was managed by three muscular slaves, who
took great pride in their skillful poling. They were
furnished with sixty pounds of bacon and two
bushels of meal for the trip, and they helped themselves to the tobacco, wheat, corn, and potatoes of
the down cargo, and the salt, coffee, sugar, molasses
and whiskey of the up cargo. As fresh fish was also
plentiful and eggs and milk could be bought along
the way, their nightly picnics under the trees on
the shore were something in the nature of festivals,
enlivened, of course, by the ubiquitous banjo.

A jolly life and picturesque touch upon the water
and the landscape, which came to an end when the
canal was built.

For in spite of the lurid romanticism of the aboli-
tionist, the slave in Virginia found many satisfactory compensations for his lot. And in spite of
the lurid realism from Harlem to-day, the average
Virginia negro still finds life more agreeable than

otherwise. He is being educated. There are ever-increasing numbers of colleges and industrial schools, many of them locally supported, and the public schools in the larger towns are comparable to the white public schools, with a nutritious hot luncheon served at noon for a few cents. There are free playgrounds for those brown children, who are surely the most irresistible of any young of the human race. There are perfectly equipped wings in the hospitals where the colored members of the community are accepted without charge, and highly sanitary whitewashed cells in the local jails where they are frequently but not unkindly retained to consider the rectification of their ways. To be sure, the most highly educated colored leaders are not content. Can a contented man be a leader? The zealous New-Englanders who shake their heads over the colored problem in the South do not exaggerate its difficulties. But perhaps they do exaggerate the practicability of their solution of it.

The Virginian is working out his own solution, in regard to a people with whom he has always lived in utmost friendliness. And he is accomplishing this as painlessly and as rapidly as is healthily possible.

CHAPTER X

LEXINGTON, THE HOME OF HEROES

AFTER having been peculiarly difficult of access for years, Lexington has recently found itself the converging point for five national highways and a favorite objective for automobilists. From whatever direction one approaches it, the country is rolling and peaceful, and suggestive, in some way that escapes definition, of the charm of an English landscape. The town, which took its name from the Revolutionary battle, retains an English flavor in its architecture and atmosphere.

Here, in this quietly isolated part of Virginia,

have lived some of the most famous constructors of American history. This was not a coincidence, but was due to the two well-known educational institutions which are situated on one of the fine upland plateaus fifteen hundred feet above sea level. As the students from Washington and Lee University live in the town, and the cadets of the Virginia Military Institute live in dormitories on their own campus, perhaps the affiliation between the town and the former is closer. But Lexington makes a point of reflecting the spirited rivalry which has always characterized the two schools. For although the campus of Washington and Lee and the parade ground of V.M.I. lie side by side without visible barrier, each is exceedingly jealous of its autonomy and regards its neighbor with uneasy contempt. This hostility — apparently based upon no more logical cause than proximity — has waxed and waned with varying intensity for a hundred-odd years. It inspired the students from Washington and Lee upon one covert and infelicitous occasion to paint the most prized possession of its enemy — the cannon — a venomous green. It inspired the cadets to return the compliment by painting the columns of the main building of their antagonists a red, white, and yellow. Turpentine and apologies were the ignominious finale of this interchange. The climax was a violent fisticuff encounter about twenty-five years ago, and a subsequent permanent sundering of athletic relations. It is difficult for the detached observer to follow the *nuances* of the lively feud. But that much overworked man from Mars might say the same about the perpetual tension existing between certain European nations. And, like their larger counterparts in hating, the two proud little institutions have much in common in spite of themselves: their lofty situation, their intimate connection with great men, and their intensely Southern feeling. Both have students from all over the country — Washington and Lee principally from the far South; both have long and honorable histories, and both rank high in the modern academic world.

The University of Washington and Lee has had almost as many changes of name as a much-married movie actress. In the early part of the eighteenth century, those vigorous Scotch-Irish immigrants who had penetrated into the valley of the Shenandoah established Augusta Academy, fifteen miles from what is now Staunton. In 1776, its name was changed to Liberty Hall, and in 1780, it was moved to the vicinity of Lynchburg and rechristened Washington Academy. A few years later, the Legislature of Virginia presented George Washington with fifty thousand dollars' worth of shares in a James River Canal company in recognition of his services during the Revolution. These he refused to accept for his own benefit, but his attention being called to the needs of Liberty Hall he presented the shares to it. 'To promote literature in this rising empire,' he politely wrote, 'and to encourage the arts have ever been among the warmest wishes of my heart.' The trustees were so overcome by this donation that they proceeded to change the name again — this time to Washington Academy. (The property thus bestowed still yields an income of about three thousand dollars a year.) Shortly after the turn of the nineteenth century, the Academy was destroyed by fire, and a new building was constructed on the present site. This became Washington College. In 1865, when General Robert E. Lee was elected president, the institution assumed its present corporate title.

While there are many worthy traditions and buildings here, what most impresses the visitor is the permeation of the entire place by the personality of the great Confederate general. It is a definite and constant sense of worshipful veneration

for one who typifies, with an appeal increasing with
the passage of time, the ideal of Southern chivalry.
While it is to be expected that the students should
lift their caps whenever they pass the Memorial
Chapel where he lies buried, it is noticeable that the
cadets from V.M.I. never fail to salute in passing
the spot. And the Episcopalians among them attend the Episcopal Church very reverently, even
though it is on the soil of their hereditary hatred.
All of this hero-worship is graphically epitomized
in Edward Valentine's impressive statue of Lee.
Recumbent in white marble in the Lee Memorial
Chapel there is something both stately and gentle
about the figure and the face. The sculptor has
caught the peculiar high attractiveness of the man's
nature, the sadness of a lost cause, and the tranced
hush of death. Below the statue is a museum, with
many pictures of Lee, not of great artistic merit,
but cumulative in the effect which they altogether
produce of his delicately vivid personal beauty. In
the crypt which holds his remains lie those of his
wife and other members of his family, and of his
father, dashing 'Light-Horse Harry.' Near the
crypt is the room which the General used as an
office and which is still kept as he left it. The house
in which he lived, and which was given him by the

people of Virginia, is now used as the residence of
the President of the University.

Virginia Military Institute came into existence
quite differently. When the Treaty of Ghent termi-
nated the War of 1812, the State of Virginia was
forced to provide for a large accumulation of arms
and ammunition. It established three arsenals, one
of them at Lexington. The garrison of this arsenal,
detailed from State troops, became a decided nui-
sance to the small Scotch Presbyterian village, and
Richmond, after considerable importuning, decided
to found a military school upon the site. Colonel
Claude Crozet, who built the Chesapeake and Ohio
tunnels under the Blue Ridge, was serving at the
time as State Engineer. A graduate of the École
Polytechnique in France, an officer in Napoleon's
army, and for several years professor of engineering
in the United States Military Academy, he was
chosen president. He modeled the fledgling institution as nearly as possible upon the lines of West
Point, recruiting his faculty, whenever he could,
from West Point graduates. V.M.I. still tenaciously maintains her likeness to her foster mother.
The uniform of the cadets is similar, and the military bearing, the precision of the drill closely comparable. There is, however, this great difference.

West Point is dedicated to the exclusive purpose of preparing candidates for the profession of arms. The President appoints these candidates from all Congressional districts, and each cadet receives a yearly salary of about eight hundred dollars — an expense borne by the taxpayers of the Nation. At V.M.I., although every diploma carries with it a commission in the R.O.T.C., only a small proportion of graduates enter the army as a profession in the time of peace. With the exception of Virginians, who receive tuition free, every cadet pays his own way. Furthermore, he is admitted, not by appointment or political machinery, but by certificate or examination. His military duties, while sufficiently exacting, do not entrench upon academic work. The Institute has participated creditably in the four wars which have occurred during its lifetime. In the Great War, nearly eighty-three per cent of all V.M.I. men were in military service, seventy-eight per cent belonging to the commissioned personnel. And the names of its graduates prove the excellence of its preparation for a civil career.

It does not take long to walk around the campus, so superbly situated above the town. We pause to see the cadets drilling in front of the barracks; to step inside Jackson Hall, dominated by Clinedinst's famous mural painting of the charge of the cadets at New Market. One of these cadets was Sir Moses Ezekiel, whose statues — one of Virginia mourning her dead, and the other of Stonewall Jackson — dignify the grounds of his Alma Mater. Perhaps the most interesting objects and certainly the most beautiful are the extraordinarily fine old French cannon which stand on the parapet. These exquisitely wrought and engraved antiques, with others of the same kind, were a gift to this country from France, and were brought over about 1781 and landed at Cumberland on the Pamunkey River. Here they were placed on flatboats and taken up the river to Hanover Court House, where Tarleton afterward destroyed a number of them. These two particular ones, which were made in 1678 and 1693 respectively, were brought to V.M.I. in 1863, while it was still an arsenal. Others, of similar make, were melted up to make cannon for the Confederate forces, and two of these are now beside the old French cannon, with name-plates showing the battles in which they were used. Even people who are not ordinarily interested in military trophies cannot but be impressed by the lavish and tasteful ornamentation of these magnificent pieces, the French *fleur de lis* enwreathing them.

Of course the outstanding figure in the history of the Institute is that of Stonewall Jackson, who was Professor of Artillery Tactics and Natural Philosophy here. The words he shouted to the Federal Army at Chancellorsville on May 2, 1863, are engraved upon the pedestal of his statue: 'The V.M.I. will be heard from to-day.'

The words were true, indeed, and V.M.I. was heard from in tones that still echo through American history. The great general received his death wound at Chancellorsville, but he stands in bronze forever in command of his old parade grounds flanked on either side by the six-pounder guns that were with his cadet battery at Manassas. Sir Moses Ezekiel carved the statue in Rome and presented it on its base of Italian tufa to his Alma Mater. The General's home is now the Jackson Memorial Hospital, maintained by the Mary Custis Lee Chapter of the Daughters of the Confederacy. His statue stands in the cemetery in the town, and on his birthday every year the cadets march there, and a cannon is fired over the grave.

The third great man with whom the town of Lexington must be associated is Matthew Fontaine Maury. It is curious that this name is not as familiar to every man, woman, and child in the United

States as that of Edison or Isaac Newton or Pasteur. For not only do his services to mankind save incalculable millions yearly, but they immediately affect the safety of every passenger and every piece of cargo that crosses the ocean, and the convenience of every human being who opens the daily newspaper to see the latest cable fron Europe or what the weather will be to-morrow. Aside from this hourly practical application of the science which he formulated, that science itself is of the most romantic nature imaginable — being nothing less than blazing a track through the hitherto unchartered winds and tides and currents of the universe. Prospero, with his wand and plummet, was a theatrical novice beside this quiet Virginia gentleman, who mapped the floor of the ocean, laid down the lanes for the ocean steamers — in brief, lifted what had up to his time been unpredictable vagaries of nature into a classified part of man's knowledge.

It is directly due to him that every ship that navigates the high seas has become 'a floating laboratory, a temple of Science.' His charts, which are among the most valuable productions of the human mind, have caused him to be regarded by many countries as the greatest man America ever produced. It is difficult for us, who accept as part

STONEWALL JACKSON'S HOUSE, NOW THE JACKSON MEMORIAL HOSPITAL

of our modern civilization the results of his tremendous labor, to realize the state of navigation pre-
vious to it. And it brings the genius of a man who
was born over a hundred years ago quite strikingly
into our present-day life to have those explorers of
the air — Byrd and Amundsen — verify the truth
of Commodore Maury's prediction as to the polar
sea.

But to begin at the beginning. Born near Fredericksburg in 1806, Matthew Fontaine Maury began his career as a midshipman, and nine years of
almost continuous sea duty — he was on the first
American man-of-war to circumnavigate the globe
— was a splendid preparation for the work which
was to make him famous. Becoming master of the
Falmouth and wishing to make the long cruise to
the Pacific as quickly as possible, he searched for
some information concerning the winds and currents and the best course for his ship to take. He
was dumfounded to discover that there was practically no such information. The observations of
these phenomena of the sea which he made on this
voyage turned his mind toward a series of such investigations and led him to the writing of his epoch-
making articles and the book which was the first
nautical work of science to come from the pen

of an American naval officer. 'A New Theoretical and Practical Treatise on Navigation' (published in 1836) promptly took the place of Bowditch's 'Practical Navigator' as a textbook for junior officers in the navy, and was favorably reviewed by the editor of the *Southern Literary Messenger* — a prophetic young man by the name of Edgar Allan Poe.

Writing, studying mineralogy, geology, astronomy, and drawing, he was promoted to the rank of lieutenant and won distinction as a hydrographer, astronomer, and surveyor.

When in 1839 he broke his leg in a stage-coach accident and was forced to give up active service at sea, the Government in recognition of his services put him in charge of the Depot of Charts and Instruments at Washington — later to be known as the United States National Observatory and Hydrographic Office. From the mass of dusty logbooks he found there, he began his stupendous compilation now known to every mariner as 'Wind and Currents Chart.' One of these combines the result of 1,159,353 separate observations on the force and direction of the wind and upward of 100,000 observations on the height of the barometer at sea. He supplemented these records by winning the coöperation of more than a thousand vessels, which collected data as they voyaged across the seven seas and sent them to him. Naturally his revelations were first met with skepticism. Map a current? Predict a cyclone? Explain why one coast is dry and another rainy? On being informed of the latitude and longitude of a spot, pronounce infallibly its prevailing weather and winds? Ridiculous! His vindication came rather spectacularly. The San Francisco, with hundreds of troops on board, foundered in an Atlantic hurricane. Rumors of its distress reached port, and Maury was called on to indicate the probable location of the breaking vessel. He immediately figured out the exact spot where the winds and currents would combine to drive a helpless wreck, and marked it with a blue pencil on a chart. Relief was dispatched to that place and the survivors found. This was absolutely the first time in the history of navigation that such a thing had occurred. From that hour to this, Maury's word has been accepted without challenge, and, on the top of every pilot chart issued by the Hydrographic Office of the Navy Department is still written: 'Founded upon the researches made and the data collected by Lieutenant M. F. Maury, U.S. Navy.'

Combined with his accuracy and passion for

scientific research, Maury had an extraordinary literary style which did a great deal toward bringing his books into public notice and making them popular as textbooks both in this country and in translated versions. One opens his 'Physical Geography of the Sea' to read: 'There is a river in the ocean. In the severest droughts it never fails and in the mightiest floods it never overflows. Its banks and its bottom are of cold water, while its current is of warm. The Gulf of Mexico is its fountain, and its mouth is in the Arctic Seas. It is the Gulf Stream. There is in the world no other such majestic flow of waters. Its current is more rapid than the Mississippi or the Amazon, and its volume more than a thousand times greater.' And in another place: 'At the dead hour of the night, when there is not a sound to be heard save the dead beat escapement of the clock counting with hollow voice the footsteps of time in his ceaseless round, I turn to the Ephemeris and find there, by calculation made years ago, that when that clock tells a certain hour, a star which I never saw will be in the field of the telescope for a moment, flit through, and then disappear. The instrument is set; — I look: the star mute with eloquence that gathers sublimity from the silence of the night comes smiling and dancing into the field, and at the instant predicted even to the fraction of a second it makes its transit and is gone.' Surely Herman Melville himself might read such passages with delight. Maury's life was crammed with events. In 1853, he instigated the United States to call the Brussels Conference for the coöperation of nations in regard to maritime affairs. It was here that he advocated the extension of meteorological observations to the land — thus founding the first weather bureau. It was his discovery of the still-water plateaus of the North Atlantic and the causes of the Gulf Stream which made possible the laying of the first Atlantic Cable. Cyrus W. Field said: 'Maury furnished the brains: England gave the money, and I did the work.'

The full and happy domestic life of this man, the honors, decorations, and degrees conferred on him by learned societies and foreign rulers, his writings, researches, and inventions, his part in the Civil War and his brief connection with Maximilian in Mexico, and his concluding years as a professor at the Virginia Military Institute have at last been presented in book form by Charles Lee Lewis, and published by the United States Naval Institute. Although he is still denied a place in the Hall of Fame, a monument is soon to be erected to him in

Richmond, and one of the buildings of the Naval Academy bears his name. And there are a few scattering and minor memorials to him throughout the South. This does not seem excessive recognition for a man whose name is one of the few engraved upon the exterior of the Seaman's Institute in Hamburg, Germany, and whose statue is over the main entrance of the Meteorological Station of the German Admiralty in Hamburg — a man for whom special medals were struck by practically every great European country.

Although Fredericksburg claims him because he was born there, and Richmond because he is buried in Hollywood Cemetery between Presidents Monroe and Taylor, he is closely and affectionately associated with V.M.I., where his house is pointed out to visitors, and where the physical sciences are taught in Maury-Brooks Hall.

The State of Virginia did, a few years ago, erect a monument in the Goshen Pass, through which his body was carried to its final burial place. The bronze tablet bears as part of its inscription:

Matthew Fontaine Maury
Pathfinder of the Seas
The Genius who first snatched
From Ocean and Atmosphere
The Secret of their Laws

But Maury's own words most movingly express his life-work and his high attitude toward it:

'So to shape the course on voyages at sea to make the most of the winds and currents is the perfection of the navigator's art. How the winds blow or currents flow along this route or that is no longer a matter of speculation or opinion. The wind and the weather, daily encountered by hundreds who sailed before him, have been tabulated for the mariner: nay, the path has been blazed for him on the sea: mile posts have been set upon the waves and time tables furnished for the trackless waste.'

CHAPTER XI

ROCKBRIDGE COUNTY PARADOXES

ROCKBRIDGE COUNTY is one of the most tranquil, unjostled stretches of country in all Virginia. Its calm meadows undulate without abruptness and pretty creeks meander down its slopes. The Blue Ridge protects it on the east and the Alleghanies on the west. It is comfortably remote from the storms of the seacoast. It seems paradoxical that this quiet bit of countryside should produce two startling phenomena, one in stone — the great Natural Bridge — and the other in flesh, Cyrus Hall McCormick.

There is a comfortable brick farmhouse in Rock-bridge County, eighteen miles south of Staunton. Here was born in 1809 a child whose father was a farmer, a weaver, a student of astronomy, and the inventor of many agricultural machines. His mother was Scotch-Irish — a woman of great energy and mentality. Near the farmhouse is a field which rolls to the rim of an idyllic rivulet. In this field that child — when a young man — tested the machine with which he, like his father before him, had been struggling for years, using the black-smith's shop on the place for his workroom. This machine was a reaper, the first that had ever been made in any country, and destined to become the breadmaker for half the human family.

Wheat has been known for fifty centuries to be man's best food. Yet until that reaper cut its first uncertain swath across the McCormick field, wheat was only available to the fortunate few — to kings and nobility in Europe, to the well-to-do in this country. Why? Not because it was especially difficult to grow, but because of the peculiar diffi-culty of its harvesting. For no matter how much grain a man may plant, he is forced to reap it all in ten days. Up to the time of the reaper, there was only one way to gather it — a way which had been used for five thousand years — the sickle and the scythe. One man with his wife to help him could, if he worked rapidly, gather enough for ten people for a year. It is obvious that no matter how great a quantity was grown, there could never be enough for every one. It was impossible to store any appreciable amount against famine. Millions of men, whose backs were bent with toiling in the wheat fields, never had enough of it to eat themselves or enough to supply their own families. When the reaper, with its self-binder, was made available, it immediately became possible for one man to cut and bind, in the same brief season, enough to feed four hundred people!

It is almost impossible for us to envision the change this has made over the entire surface of the globe. Countries which were already wheat-producing increased their crops fifty fold. Other countries began to grow crops for the first time. Whole systems of transportation were evolved on land and sea. The first wheat ship sailed around Cape Horn to California in 1860. Now the barges and steamships on canals, rivers, and oceans cannot be counted. The same was true of the railroad which came along just at the right time to help distribute this commodity. Furthermore, an entirely new type of architecture was necessitated. No one had dreamed of a grain elevator accommodating six million bushels. Before the reaper, a few barns were quite sufficient to store whatever grain was not immediately eaten. And following all these tremendous innovations came the Exchange — a world-wide news bureau, plainly stating the visible supply of wheat in the world; telling of rust in the Argentine or locusts in Siberia, a bumper crop in Roumania or a million newly ploughed acres in Canada. It is impossible for the human mind to grasp at once the gigantic implications of these changes and achievements over all the known surface of the globe. And they were directly brought about by the laboriously worked-out machine of a young Scotch-Irish boy who was a practical farmer before he was an inventor.

McCormick decided on Chicago as the most central point in which to manufacture his reaper and to distribute it. Chicago at this time had ten thousand inhabitants, who lived in rickety, unpainted shanties. It had no railroad, telegraph, gas, or sewer. However, he moved there, and ultimately he was joined by his mother and by his brothers, who had made suggestions for the reaper during the period of its invention, and who shared in the business organization and profits. But although Chicago became their home, the family always kept an affection for Virginia. The Observatory which James Leander McCormick presented to the University of Virginia, and gifts to Washington and Lee are among their substantial remembrances to the State of their birth.

The same placid country which produced this dynamo of a man produced the spectacular Natural Bridge, that phenomenon in stone which is two hundred and fifteen feet high, a hundred feet wide, and spans ninety feet of deep ravine. It is formed of a single block of Jonesboro limestone, and is of exceptional grace and symmetry.

The bold sides of the cliff of which it is a part are green with lichens, and, in the spring, bright with flowering shrubs and thousands of delicately quivering columbines. Leading to it and around it are woodland paths, each with its name and its little store of anecdote. There were two men who visited this spot under similar conditions, and their reactions were characteristic of their dispositions. The first was George Washington, who as surveyor to Lord Fairfax came upon this amazing curiosity. We can imagine him regarding it with that dispassionate air which informs every statue and picture we possess of him, as he pronounced: 'Here is a sight every lover of nature should view.'

Another man visited Natural Bridge in 1774. He was destined to be President of the United States, and his name was Thomas Jefferson. As the astonishing arch sprang across his vision, he was roused to such enthusiasm that he insisted upon surveying it with his own hands. The next year he returned, bringing two negro slaves. For them he built a two-room cabin, explicitly directing that one room should be reserved for the entertainment of strangers, fired, as he always was, by the conviction that the 'people' should have free access to every possible enjoyment. Thus it was, that standing upon the selfsame spot gazing at the selfsame phenomenon, Washington was moved to dignified utterance, and Jefferson to impetuous and idealistic action.

It is to be regretted that the latter's policy for keeping the bridge perpetually for the people has not been followed. A third chapter of our story might add that private individuals have acquired Natural Bridge, and although they have installed a system of artificial lighting so that it can be seen by night as well as by day, they have also raised a high fence along the road so that any one who wishes to see the curious formation at any time must pass out a dollar at the entrance lodge.

Quietly rolling Rockbridge County seems far removed from the turmoil of the great world. And yet here was born the man who did more than any other individual to redeem earth's richness to humanity and to abolish famine. Here lived and died another who mapped the ocean and brought it under human control. And here arches a perpetual symbol of the union between heavenly space and our terrestrial globe.

Part III
UP THE SHENANDOAH VALLEY

CHAPTER XII

THE ROAD TO STAUNTON

A MOTORIST who had toured the length and breadth of the United States passed, for the first time, over the Blue Ridge Mountains at that point where the Rockfish Valley, intensified by a hundred rolling hills, stretches out into apparent infinity. Dumfounded by the breath-taking quality of this panorama, he sought out a Virginian acquaintance.

'Man alive!' he exclaimed, 'don't you realize you have a view here as magnificent as any in America! If this valley were in California, it would be advertised all over the world.'

The Virginian shrugged his shoulders ever so slightly.

'Would you like us to be like Californians?' he asked.

Perhaps this retort illustrates the attitude of the Virginian better than it does the Rockfish Valley. There is no State in the Union more keenly aware of its beauties and of its historical wealth. And there is no State which makes less effort to exploit them. Why try to corral hurrying tourists into your country when really you prefer privacy? Why spend your life encouraging industries and making money when you already have all the satisfactions of happy environment and leisure to enjoy it and the jolliest kind of social life with your kin and your kind?

But the omnivorous automobilist has no intention of keeping out of Virginia merely because he has not happened to receive an urgent and personal invitation to visit it. Every year hundreds of astonished strangers discover that the forty-one-mile ride from Charlottesville to Staunton is one of the most spectacular in the country. Those who are staying in Charlottesville without their own car will find that the bus travels the same road in great comfort.

The drive starts out modestly enough, leaving the University behind, and passing by red-brick houses with white pillars, set high on the hill, and many others which are only indicated by the handsome entrance gates. On either side of the excellent road are banks of that red clay whose color gives such richness to the landscape. Honeysuckle grows like mad, all along the edges, and on the side of the rolling hills undulate immense patches of Scotch broom, a dazzling sheet of gold in the spring and a strong vibrant green throughout the rest of the year. Jefferson, who had yearly importations from the Jardin des Plantes for his own gardens at Monticello, brought the broom to Virginia, thinking it would prevent gullies in the hillsides. So it does, but it also drives the farmer to profanity and the artist into raptures by its strong and brilliant persistence.

The settlements are small, far apart, and shabby. Here and there one sees an old-fashioned well with a bucket, a graveyard with two or three forlorn stones, and, as we approach Crozet, more and more apple and peach orchards, unfolding, in season, into clouds of pink-and-white blossoms. Crozet, which still keeps its French pronunciation, was named for the Colonel Crozet who was the first President of

V.M.I., and who constructed the Chesapeake and Ohio tunnel under the Blue Ridge. Now the name is synonymous, in the fruit world, with apples, for Crozet is a great apple center, as its conspicuous cold-storage warehouses testify. It is the home of the famous Albemarle Pippin, which for almost a century has been the favorite with the reigning house of England and for that reason was politely exempted from tariff.

As we pass through Crozet, the view becomes more extended and the looming mountains are outlined more distinctly. We pass Mirador, the girlhood home of Lady Astor, and farther on the arcaded Emmanuel Church, remodeled by Lady Astor and her brothers and sisters as a memorial to their mother, Mrs. Langhorne. The mountains continue to rise higher and higher. Fences crisscross the pastures defining the paddocks: peach and apple orchards are patterned against the slopes and in the valleys. Occasionally we pass a dignified entrance gate. We cannot see the house at the far end of the winding drive, which is our loss and the inhabitants' gain. Virginians have never been afraid of living in isolation — if being surrounded by a large family and a perpetual house party of relatives, guests, plenty of servants, and saddle horses, to say nothing of motor cars in these modern days, can be called isolation. Just before we begin to ascend the mountain, we notice that the car slows down unaccountably. The same instinct which at one time would have declared that a widdershin had been drawn here, or a witch buried, now insists that there is a magnetic attraction here — an undiscoverable lodestone — which affects the motor. But the unromantic truth is that at this spot the grade deceives the eye.

And now we begin to climb up toward Afton, by long hairpin curves, while below us the Rockfish Valley unrolls and unrolls like an enchanted scroll, the road lying across it like an untied ribbon. Moses, looking out far over the Promised Land, saw nothing more splendid than this . . .

As soon as we have topped the mountain, with its Swannanoa Clubhouse, and begun the descent into Augusta County, we notice a difference in temperature. The dwellers on the Piedmont side of the Blue Ridge are very emphatic also about the many other differences. They explain that, while their section was settled by the English Cavaliers, this section we are now entering was settled by the Scotch-Irish and Dutch, which has profoundly affected all of its subsequent habits, culture, and

appearance. To the stranger this tremendous difference is not immediately apparent. But the
Virginians have always been sectionalists. A
volume could be compiled on the variations in
speech and custom which persist in the different
regions. Where but in Tidewater does one speak of
a 'mantua-maker' for a dressmaker, and where
outside of Bedford County is the disrespectful 'Did
you ever get left' expressed in a sibilant 'Ab-a-
sicci.' The dwellers in the Shenandoah Valley refer
to the inhabitants of Piedmont with withering
contempt as 'Tuckahoes.' Passionate arguments
concerning these points prove they are no trifling
matter. Tidewater Virginia is rather patronizing
toward Piedmont Virginia, and both of them as-
sume great airs toward the Valley. Since we are
about to enter Staunton, which is the gateway to
the Shenandoah Valley, perhaps it is well to remember that the Scotch-Irish struck the first note of the
Revolution when they issued the Declaration of
Mecklenburg. They gave Washington thirty-nine
of his generals, three out of four members of his
Cabinet, and three out of five judges of the first
Supreme Court. John Fiske called them 'the main
strength of our American democracy,' and Bancroft
reminds us that 'the first voice publicly raised to

dissolve all connection with Great Britain came, not from the Puritans of New England, or the Dutch of New York, or the planters of Virginia, but from the Scotch-Irish Presbyterians.'

It is not wholly a coincidence, therefore, that the most interesting spot in Staunton is the birthplace of a certain Scotch-Irish Presbyterian named Woodrow Wilson. This birthplace still serves its original purpose as the manse for the First Presbyterian Church — a sufficiently comfortable house, without any undue lavishness about it, which in the day of its famous occupant possessed much more extensive grounds.

Although Staunton is the county seat of Augusta County, so conservatively do the stores range themselves along the downtown streets, and so unobtrusively do the pleasant homes on the hill settle down in the midst of their gardens, that it is easy for the motorist to rush through the city without paying particular attention to anything beyond a good meal at the new hotel or a foray into one of the numerous antique shops.

But the city is worthy of more interest. It received both the spelling of its name and its pronunciation (which is 'Stanton') from Lady Staunton, wife of Governor Gooch. The extent of the county in early Colonial days was such that once court was adjourned to meet at Fort Duquesne — or what is now the city of Pittsburgh! According to the Virginia London Company's Grant in 1609, Staunton was the capital of a territory that reached from the Atlantic to the Pacific.

It is mentioned as a town first in 1748, when forty-four town lots were laid off, each containing about half an acre. The streets running east and west were named Beverley, Frederick, and Johnson, and those running north and south Augusta, Water, and Lewis. In giving possession of these lots the old English custom of 'livery of seizin' was practiced, the commissioners and purchasers going on the premises together, and the former passing to the latter a handful of earth in token of the delivery of the whole.

The inhabitants of Staunton showed good sense and good taste recently in giving back to its modern Main Street the original name of Beverley. For Beverley and Augusta have always been famous thoroughfares — the stage, in fact, for nearly all of Staunton's history. Before the removal of the Southern Indians west of the Mississippi, Staunton was on the direct route from their country to Washington, and Cherokees and Chickasaws and

Choctaws frequently passed through on their way to visit the Great Father.

The Knoxville teams were a great sight, too, a hundred years ago. The East Tennessee merchants transported their goods from Baltimore by huge covered wagons, and every spring was heralded by a stream of lumbering wains, drawn by horses decked with bells. After the extension of the James River Canal to Lynchburg, the picturesque teams disappeared. The mail coaches afforded some excitement, however, and in 1833 the flood of emigration from Eastern Virginia and North Carolina surged through, pioneering men and tired women, yellow-haired children and dogs — all bound for Ohio.

Another annual procession was composed of huge droves of swine being driven up from Kentucky to some market beyond Staunton. Small carts, drawn by small horses, bringing sweet potatoes from Nelson County and oysters from Fredericksburg, were part of the scene.

But the most thrilling period was during the 'Springs season' when the stage-coaches and private carriages with horses and liveried servants passed through Staunton on their way to the various Virginia Springs. The Baltimore Bonapartes always made a tremendous stir. A small boy stationed as an outpost would cry, 'Bonaparte is coming!' and every one would run to a door or window to look out. First would come a buggy drawn by two horses, in which sat one or two elegant gentlemen. Next came the family carriage drawn by four horses and carrying the ladies and children. Then a two-horse spring wagon with the baggage. Thus with three vehicles, ten horses, and sundry servants the nephew of Napoleon made his entry and passed through the streets.

Being fifteen hundred feet above sea level, Staunton is peculiarly healthy, which may partly account for its selection and success as an educational center. There are nine well-known private schools here, one college, one State school.

The chapel where Woodrow Wilson's father used to preach is still to be seen — now part of the Mary Baldwin Seminary. And on an exhilarating hilltop are drilling six or seven hundred boys, each of them, thanks to his cap and uniform, a neat replica of the lad we have seen for years in the magazines advertising the Staunton Military Academy. A large insane asylum and deaf and dumb school are likewise here, housed in buildings of unusual architectural merit.

STAUNTON

In the front yard of Trinity Church, just to the left of the entrance gate, is a plaque which commemorates the meeting of the Virginia Assembly here, June 7–23, 1781. The Assembly had abandoned Richmond on May 1, and adjourned to Charlottesville to escape the British. In Charlottesville on June 4, Jack Jouett warned it of Tarleton's approach, and it hastily adjourned to meet in Staunton in the old Parish House which stood upon the site of this tablet on which the list of its members is recorded.

Behind Trinity, a short way down Church Street, is a red-brick house with white pillars. Jefferson was a great friend of the family who lived here — and whose descendants still live here — and to him is ascribed the plan of the house. Certainly the delicate detail over the front and side doors, the circular window, and the fine gateway are suggestive of the man who is at last coming into recognition as one of America's greatest architects.

It is true of all towns, but particularly so in the South, that their individuality is only revealed by leisurely and prolonged acquaintance. Over ninety per cent of the population of Staunton is Augusta County native-born, American stock, including the 13.2 per cent of the colored race; so, in spite of its prosperous manufacturing industries, it does not have the problems of foreign-born labor. Perhaps the homogeneous racial stock also accounts for Staunton's being the first city in the country to adopt the commission form of government — the city manager form — which it did in 1908.

Those of us who have seen large industrial cities are not particularly interested in Staunton's quite legitimate claim to consideration along these lines. It is the climate and tenacious fidelity to tradition which mark it for us. We are glad that Main Street has resumed the name of Beverley, and glad that Gospel Hill is still designated so, although the clergy no longer live upon its neighborly slope.

CHAPTER XIII

HARRISONBURG AND THE VALLEY

STAUNTON is the southern and Winchester the northern entrance to the Shenandoah Valley. Between these two cities is a third — Harrisonburg. There is no drive in the entire length and breadth of our immense United States more lovely than these two hundred miles, comprising the fertile pastures and bright rivers of thirteen counties, lying between the Blue Ridge Mountains on the east and the Alleghanies on the west. This road which our automobiles skim over so swiftly to-day is almost the identical route which the feet of the red men beat as a war trail; it is the same highway that the youthful George Washington surveyed in the days when he was employed by Lord Fairfax; it is the 'good broad highway leading down' which 'like an arrowy Alpine river flowed' under the spurning hoofs of Sheridan's steed, 'a steed as black as the steeds of night' and ever dear to the tongue of the elocutionist.

The Valley has suffered all the fearful blessings of civilization since the white men took it from the Indians. Long before the Civil War raged up and down this fertile channel, each army battling for possession of the 'granary of the Confederacy,' the early settlers had felled magnificent stretches of forest trees, rolled them into heaps, and burned them to make way for corn and tobacco fields. After the Civil War towns grew up along the newly constructed railroads, and timber was ruthlessly razed for sawmills, leaving desolate ridges and slopes. To cap the damage done by tanneries, paper mills, and dye plants, which poured their poison wastes into the streams, the sportsman dynamited the creeks and trapped the few remaining game animals. Forest fires were yearly occurrences. In 1911, Congress passed a law providing for the purchase of

THE SHENANDOAH VALLEY

mountain lands for the protection of the water-sheds of navigable streams. Now more and more land is being placed under the National Forest Administration. Scientific forestry is being practiced, with its resultant increase in marketable timber. The Shenandoah National Forest owns 370,000 acres in Virginia (430,000 in Virginia and West Virginia) and the Shenandoah Park owns 327,000 acres — all to be permanently conserved. And in the meanwhile the Valley has, with the tremendous forgiveness of fecundity, obliterated the ugly scars of war, of commercialism, and wanton destruction. On the rolling bluegrass pastures white sheep and black-legged lambs are grazing: in the lee of yellow haystacks lie tranquil brown cattle. White-fenced paddocks crisscross the green fields, and the pedigreed horses for which the region is famous are housed in big gambrel-roofed stables, with equine pictures naïvely adorning their façades. Nearer the prosperous dwellings are long, well-built, well-kept poultry-houses, their yards billowy with white fowls. Clear green streams form boundary lines to the wheat fields and orchards, and circle around old mansions set far back from the road and half hidden by their shrubbery. They turn and twinkle under the bridges of the scattering towns, where women in sunbonnets pause to smile at the passer-by.

As we drive along the smooth highway, these idyllic scenes unroll perpetually on either side. Beyond them, to the right, march swiftly with us the Blue Ridge Mountains. To the left, farther away, fold the peaks and slopes of the Alleghanies. What has earth to offer her children better than this? The Dutch from Pennsylvania discovered the fertility of this valley at the beginning of the eighteenth century and their impress is still clearly discernible. The big brick houses, with their double chimneys at either end, are reminiscent of similar architecture throughout Pennsylvania. Although Harrisonburg holds up the Virginia standard of ninety-eight per cent native-born population, the faces of the people on her streets and the names over the shop doors retain more than a trace of those German ancestors. In fact, if one will turn off the main highway from Harrisonburg, and push his way four miles into the hills, he will come to a certain hamlet where German is still spoken in many homes, and where instead of listening to the radio friends and neighbors meet to sing and to play together in quartet and *ensemble*. This is Dayton, where the Shenandoah College carries a rather re-

markable curriculum in music, has supported its
own music publishing house for three generations,
and has worked out its own system of musical no-
tation by which even the beginning amateur can
play a piece of music in any key he chooses without consciously transposing. Here, on New Year's
Day, a festival is held, in which a thousand singers
join in perfectly blended chorus. 'But where does
the audience sit?' asks the visitor, glancing at the
church in which the festival is held. 'Oh, there is
no audience,' he is told. 'Every one is singing.'

There are other places, sleeping behind these
folded hills, for the tourist who makes Harrisonburg
headquarters, and who has time to leave the beaten
track. The home of Abraham Lincoln's grand-
father still stands, very much as it was when Lincoln visited it during his Presidency.

But the most extraordinary excursion from
Harrisonburg is not on the surface of the earth at
all, but underneath it — a subterranean excursion
and well worth the attention of every traveler. For
the limestone, whose disintegration has wrought
the fertility of this whole valley, has also wrought
a miracle below the soil. A brook, carving its first
shallow bed at the level of the Laurentian Plain,
pursuing a course no one can calculate how many

eons ago, gradually seeped down between the rocks, wore away the soluble limestone, and became a subterranean river. Burrowing deeper and deeper, it left behind corridors and galleries, caves and labyrinths of endless extent and of a formation which seems the apotheosis of modernist sculpture. One cannot say how many of these cities of silence lie below the surface of the Valley, or how closely they interpenetrate each other. But so many of them have been opened, made accessible to the public, and furnished with guides and cleverly illuminated by indirect lighting, that the traveler through the Valley can stop at the time most convenient to his own plans and be sure of seeing something he will never forget. The most jaded sightseer will find such a stop worth his while, for the strange petrified scenes have never been sullied by the smoke of torches and are revealed in the pristine rose and blue, the cream and bronze of the water-eroded stone. Some of the corridors and lofty vestibules are elaborate with muddy colors and heavy forms that remind us of a German Kurhaus. In others long streamers, exquisitely tinted and semi-transparent, are folded and pleated in symmetrical regularity. Some of these moulded rocks, during the ages of their formation, were so incessantly played upon by a current of air that they are twisted into long graceful petals. There are rooms that suggest tropical forests, and others that have the arches of Oriental mosques. There are miniature kingdoms of glittering white columns around lakes of crystal clarity. Some of the sculpture is brutal, and follows unaccustomed laws of proportion, balance, or line. Other forms are airily and lightly chiseled, with extravagant loveliness, and ingrained with fanciful coloring.

The mind that is able to appreciate anything only in terms of something else will find great satisfaction in tracing out resemblances, and in eagerly identifying those already traced out by former visitors of similar imagination. Frying-pans and elephant ears, boiled eggs and broken-down buggies can all be discerned amid these sublime and terrifying phenomena. Even so the Taj Mahal may be likened to a wedding cake, and the wedding cake to a snowdrift, and the snowdrift, in turn, to the Taj Mahal.

But even the volubility of such commentators cannot ruin the weird wonder of the caverns. Here, where the temperature never varies, not with day or night, not with the changing seasons, not even with the slow roll of the centuries; here where, except at moments when the electric illumination is turned on, exists forever a darkness impenetrable and absolute — we are in a universe incomparable to any other. Imagine the silence in these rock-walled chambers as the last human footstep echoes away.

> 'I shall not see the shadows,
>   I shall not feel the rain;
> I shall not hear the nightingale
>   Sing on, as if in pain,'

sighs Christina Rossetti, from her musical, shadowy grave.

But this crypt, so far below the sun, holds a silence deeper than even Christina could imagine. For even the deepest grave which hides the profoundest mystery has once been open to the light. But these tombs are irrevocably beyond all earthly vibrations. To pass through them is to pass completely out of this world. And to emerge from them is to come miraculously back from Pluto's grim and dreadful and magnificent domain to life — to happiness and peace and quiet breathing.

The world is warm and pulsing and friendly as we come out into it again. How much more agreeable to tend a humble flock of hens, for instance, in the sunshine, than a flock of bats in the most splendid ballroom of the Grottoes! And the commonest apples lying on the ground are more appetizing than those bronze ones which garland the walls of the forever mute banquet hall!

The road bounds blithely out into the sunshine, and now the long level wall of the Massanutten Mountains begins to march along with us. Antique shops are cunningly placed to lure us into stopping, and every other house waves a sign assuring us that tourists are welcome.

They have always been welcome along the Valley. In 1774, the traveler could get a warm meal for sixpence and a cold one for fourpence. There were no gas stations, to be sure, but stablage for one's horse, fodder, pasturage, or a gallon of corn or oats was fourpence. A servant had a lower-priced 'diet' than his master. Lodging was three-pence, with careful explanation that a feather bed cost more than a straw tick, and two or three in a bed might claim reduction in rates. Yes, the Valley has had a long training in accommodating the passer-by. And should you happen to find some detail of your table service not entirely satisfactory, console yourself by remembering that when Louis-Philippe, King of France, with his two ducal brothers, of Montpensier and Beaujolais, were refugees

in this country in 1796, they once stopped at a
Valley inn. When they asked that their dinner be
sent to their rooms, they were informed by an in-
dignant and democratic host that they could come
to the common table or proceed on their journey
dinnerless! Valley folk have always been unawed
by foreign swank.

We come to New Market, where the V.M.I. cadets
— children we should call them to-day, for some of
them were only fourteen years old — rushed forth
to fight, to lose their lives, to win a victory over
Federal troops in one of the most spirited and
heart-breaking encounters of all history. It had
its laughable side, too, that battle of New Market,
for the Northerners were, for the moment, completely bewildered by the sudden appearance of
these diminutive and lively figures, and could not
imagine what manner of Lilliputian enemy was so
amazingly confronting them. A few years ago one
hundred and fifty thousand spectators witnessed a
sham battle on the selfsame spot, in which the
V.M.I. cadets participated against thirty-five hundred United States Marines under Brigadier General Smedley D. Butler. Grass grows quickly over
battle-scarred soil. Old wounds heal, and the markers and monuments all along the road are worded
without rancor.

We pass various towns. Mount Jackson, Edinburg, and Woodstock were trading-posts in the days when Daniel Boone traveled up and down the Valley. It was in Woodstock that Peter Muhlenberg, a Lutheran minister, preached a dramatic sermon in 1775, at the close of which he threw off his black ministerial robe and revealed his military uniform beneath. 'There is a time to preach, a time to pray, and a time to fight,' he shouted, and called for volunteers. More than three hundred signed at once.

If it happens to be Saturday night as we come to Woodstock, we will find the main street milling with men and women and children from the rural districts and the mountains. The local jail is socially crowded with temporary tenants who stand at the open barred windows singing in loud, cheerful, albeit somewhat unsteady tones. Should it happen to be Sunday, such quietness pervades shop and house that we will be sure that Sabbath calm is the portion of the inhabitants all the days of the week.

If one has an hour to spare, he cannot do better than to turn off, opposite the old courthouse at Woodstock, and take the winding way to the Observation Tower. Every sweep of this admirably laid-out road, rising and curving with the ascent of the mountain, reveals a gorgeous vista of the long wide Valley below. The road enters the Shenandoah National Forest and leads finally to a crude wooden observation tower from which the spectator can look down over a stupendous panorama. The forested mountains form two blue parallel walls. Between them lies the fertile Valley, through which the river makes seven perfect loops of unvarying width and almost artificial regularity. Each of these loops is evenly edged with verdure and encircles a farm and its outbuildings, their red roofs and white walls gleaming through the green. As far as the eye can reach, the neatly patterned fields and orchards lie in green and tawny and rosy patches. With glasses the Washington Monument is visible, over a hundred miles away. If one should travel by river, he would find the distance forty-five miles between the same points that the road makes in seven.

Where we are standing, the Indian must often have stood, and he looked out upon a prospect which was very much as it is to-day. Instead of automobiles, the moccasined feet of Shawnees, Delawares, Catawbas, and Dacotahs passed and repassed over the wide war trail. Instead of rifle and reel, the sportsman was carrying ash bows and flint arrows, and stone tomahawks bound into their wooden hunting-handles by deerskin thongs. Smoke rose from fires in the Valley below where the women were cooking wolf, fox, otter, and beaver or drying them for the winter's supply. In season, corn and nuts and honey were harvested, and the maple sap cooled and stored. Baskets were woven and pottery fashioned and painted, fur cured for garments, and bright feathers woven into headdresses. The Valley was not wooded even at this time, for the red men had discovered that buffalo would leave the forest to seek the clear spaces, and therefore it was the custom, at the end of each hunting season, to fire the grass. By opening new pastures the range of the buffalo herds and also that of elk and deer was extended and a new supply of food secured. With the coming of the white immigrant down from the Potomac, this custom of firing ceased.

The Indian has gone and so has the buffalo. Civilized man fell upon them and wrought depredations upon the smiling Valley at which the savage stood aghast. He saw the pale-faced conquerors ravage the timber, poison the brooks, decimate the wild creatures of forest and stream, and pursue his own brother up and down the length of the Valley to slaughter him. The Indian did not stay to see how, after two centuries, the white man has gradually approached rationality, how he is seeking to preserve what he once sought to destroy. Strasburg changed hands twenty-two times in one day. Cedar Creek is the point reached by Sheridan on that wild ride down from Winchester. At Kernstown can be seen the only battlefields where Stonewall Jackson's troops were not victorious. These things can never be forgotten by men, but nature forgets. The fields of Carthage were sowed with salt so that they would never bear again. But to-day those hills are smoothly green and sheep and lambs are grazing on them. Even so the Shenandoah Valley has burgeoned. Birds are daring to return. Fish are darting in the river, and wheat fields and orchards and wide roads bear witness to earth's reconciliation with man.

CHAPTER XIV

WINCHESTER AND THE NEW SOUTH

THE tendency to idealize the past, which is inherent in most of us, has been lavishly indulged by the South. It was inevitable that the survivors of the most leisurely and graceful civilization that this country has ever known should lament its painful, its humiliating destruction. But the habit of lamentation did not begin with the Civil War. Read the following: 'In whose hands now are the once proud seats of Westover, Cerles, Maycoks,

Shirley . . . ? They have passed into other and stranger hands. Some of the descendants of illustrious parentage have gone to the far West, while others, lingering behind, have contrasted their present condition with that of their venerated ancestors. They behold themselves excluded from their fathers' houses, now in the hands of those who were once their fathers' overseers, or sinking into decay.'

This dismal survey was not clipped from the local Virginia newspaper of the current year, although it might have been. It was uttered by no less a statesman than Henry Clay in 1833. This attitude is perhaps akin to the British one. 'The London *Times* isn't what it used to be,' sadly remarks an Englishman. 'No, and it never was,' his friend suggests. The British have not noticeably lost their grip, although for centuries they have been telling each other that 'England is going to the dogs.' And so, although the South has long and loyally regretted the vanished pomps of the generation before, it has nevertheless retained more gayety, more innate response to gentle customs, more spontaneous humor, both delicate and Rabelaisian, than any other section of this country. Sometime a statistician will gather figures to prove that there are more happy people in Virginia than in any other equal area of the globe.

It is rather a pity that a State which has so much to offer should persist in emphasizing not only traditions, but distorted ones. Lost causes and a vanished social order, the vivid contrast between mountaineer and aristocrat, between faithful slave and 'ornery' poor white, the picturesque setting of the semi-feudal plantation — these have been materials irresistible to the writer of lush historical romance and to the untrained historian. Together they have produced a synthetic and flamboyant Virginia gentleman who lacked either the reality or the freshness of other American types such as the Indian, the Puritan, the frontiersman, the California miner, the Texas cowboy, or the New England spinster. This legendary Cavalier, with his incomparably beautiful lady and magnificent baronial estate, was invariably placed in a Golden Age that has already passed. John Esten Cooke wrote of the Revolutionary period which had existed before his birth. Thomas Nelson Page idealized as the Golden Age the one in which Cooke lived. Except in Thackeray's 'Virginians,' which is surprisingly accurate despite its sketchiness, the only current literature which dealt with Colonial current conditions was ill-natured satire from England — such as the Elizabethan drama which loved to ridicule the whole Colonial enterprise, or moralistic pratings from New England. The abolitionists from the North knew nothing of the South by actual contact. They contented themselves with picturing the planter as a cruel tyrant breaking the backs and hearts of his thousand cringing slaves. The Southerner retaliated by dismissing all New-Englanders as a race of peddlers, and by drawing more and more freely upon highly colored family fiction for his stories of Southern life — in which all Virginians were important members of the English nobility. It is noticeable that until comparatively few years ago there were — for all we can learn from Southern fiction — no 'second' families — except those that emigrated to North Carolina.

The pity of this perfervid and meretricious idealization has been that it obscured not only the truth, but the unique and genuine charm of Virginian civilization. It is impossible to overstate the enchantment of this sun-drenched and mountain-encircled State; impossible to be insusceptible to the spell of its winning people, its light touch and its leisurely habit of life. But it is only too possible —

as Southern literature proves — to smear the whole
subject with a sentimentality that is false and un-
attractive.

Virginia created the one genuine aristocracy
which this country has known or is likely to know.
But she did not create it because her pioneer settlers were the offspring of a dull English nobility.
The aristocracy grew out of the conditions of life —
out of the very soil and climate. That was what
made it legitimate, powerful, and unique.

Thoughtful students of early conditions in the
South are at last placing at our disposal the dispassionate facts out of which a truer and far more
entrancing legend of Virginia may perhaps evolve.
The reader is referred to 'Patrician and Plebeian in
Virginia,' by T. J. Wertenbaker, and 'Virginia
Life in Fiction,' by Jay B. Hubbell. They tell us
that at first it was the homespun simplicity of the
planter's life that distinguished it. The first planter
was a leisurely farmer: not a baron, nor a prince,
nor even a country squire. He lived in a rambling
wooden house, not in a mansion, and his 'luxury
consisted in the numerous ragged and inefficient
servants who attended him, and in the abundance
of home-grown provisions — watermelons, apple
cider, mint juleps, country ham, roasting ears, and

"snaps."' The plantation was enormous — the wealthier men possessing from four to six thousand acres. Their wasteful system of planting, without rotation of crops or use of artificial fertilizer, necessitated the continual abandonment of the exhausted fields and the taking up of fresh ones. The dignity of being a landowner on such a tremendous scale inevitably ennobled the planter's character. His way of life developed the capacity to command: to make large decisions.

The extent of these plantations was so great that the planter and his family and his slaves came to live in an isolation comparable to that of the feudal barons of the thirteenth century. This intensified the importance of family life and raised women to a more precious status. It also, in lieu of urban centers, developed the country recreations of the hunt and the house party. The entire country along the coast — where the first settlers were — was interpenetrated by rivers and inlets deep enough to float the vessels of that period. Therefore each planter had his own wharf and shipped his tobacco directly from his own estate, and received his foreign importations in the same direct manner. It was this system which was responsible for the lack of towns in Virginia during the seventeenth century. It was only when settlers began to push west beyond the region of the direct waterways that the goods had to be transported overland and roads were made perforce.

Remembering this fundamental civilization — based upon economic fact — it is easy to see how a proud, rich, and solid aristocracy had its inception. High standards of chivalry, homes that were always hospitable and in time luxurious were the legitimate results of this splendid isolation. It was not chance that four out of the first five Presidents of the United States were Virginia planters. Everything in that life had tended to produce men with the ability to command.

It is curious that the Southerner has preferred to base his undeniable aristocratic traits upon the claim that his ancestors were titled Englishmen. Not only have recent investigations proved that comparatively few of the first Virginia settlers originated from such a stratum, but it was not this few which exclusively wrought the glory of their adopted land. It would seem more inspiring to claim the truth that his forbears were men of imagination, self-confidence, and broad ambition; that they accumulated wealth and spent it with mannerly ease; that the women developed that grace conferred by scarcity of numbers and masculine cherishing, and the executive ability demanded by their positions as mothers of large families, and châtelaines over households of enormous size, and, in time, of great elegance.

There is no question of Virginia's aristocracy being both authentic and romantic. It is only to be regretted that its least interesting factors have been overemphasized by misguided writers.

But a change is noticeable, both in the present-day literature about the South and in Southerners themselves. Progressive and ambitious men are in control of politics and education. The Governor, the President of the Chamber of Commerce, the leading editors and bankers of the State are conspicuously youthful. They are trebling Virginia's banking resources. Agriculture, good roads, and public schools are being encouraged and supported. Virginia's wealth has increased a hundredfold during the last decade, and now Texas alone of all the Southern States surpasses her.

Winchester, which is the second oldest city in the State, is an inspiring example of this healthy vitality. It is an historic city, to be sure. It was named after the capital city of Alfred the Great, to which it has a certain physical resemblance: the

English city is encircled by chalk hills and the
Virginian one by limestone, and the two have always maintained a connection of sentiment. In
1899, when the statue of Alfred the Great was dedicated in Winchester, England, the mayor and alder-
men of Winchester, Virginia, were invited to be
present. After the World War, the English Winchester presented the Virginia Winchester with the
flag which hangs in the rotunda of the Handley
Library.

She has traditions going back beyond her founding by Joseph Wood two centuries ago. They date
from Indian times, for Winchester was built upon
the site of an Indian village, where the Shawnees
had selected a spot with a good spring and a protected exposure. The Indians invariably displayed
good judgment in selecting sites for villages. Wherever the mound-builders of the Mississippi Valley
had villages, there in most cases is a modern city
or town. The history of this particular village
which is now Winchester, beginning propitiously,
ran a full, free, and commendable course. She
battled under three different flags in seven wars.
Washington had his headquarters here, both while
he was in the employ of Lord Fairfax, and later in
1756 while he was engaged in supervising the erec-

tion of Fort Loudoun. As Lieutenant-Colonel in command of the frontier he occupied the small building, made partly of undressed limestone and partly of log, which is still preserved and marked.

Holding such strategic geographical position, Winchester was extremely important during both the Revolutionary and the Civil Wars. When we remember that it changed hands seventy-two times during the latter, we do not wonder that every block in the older sections teems with anecdote. It is not so wonderful that a cannon ball passed clear through 'Cannon Ball House' as it is that there is a wall left standing to hold the old trophy.

Many of the solid stone houses built by Hessian stonemasons remain: there are many of the brick mansions of cream white or pale lilac hue and the plain brick of *ante-bellum* days. Frame houses are more numerous here than in most Virginian cities.

While there is history enough and to spare for the most voracious antiquarian, there is a new South as well as an old one in Winchester. A conspicuous testimonial to this is the imposing Handley Library, given and endowed by Judge John Handley, of Scranton, Pennsylvania. It accommodates about twenty thousand volumes, twenty-five daily newspapers, and seventy-five magazines, and refutes the time-worn joke about a certain Virginian city which delayed unconscionably in building its public library, under the impression that all aristocrats had sufficient books in their own houses. 'But what do you do if you must look up some reference and don't happen to own the particular volume you need?' one of these citizens was asked. 'Oh, we telephone Mr. James Branch Cabell,' was the complacent response. Winchester does not need to telephone any one.

The truly splendid public school, gift of the same Judge Handley, contrasts as strongly with the ancient Virginia régime where gentlemen's children were tutored at home and no one bothered much about the children of ordinary folk.

This handsome building stands upon seventy-two acres near the Valley Pike, its architecture suggestive of that most famous of all Virginian buildings — the University. With sufficient funds for modern equipment and for adequate maintenance, with an auditorium that seats fifteen hundred, gymnasium, indoor play court, nature-study court, classrooms for domestic science and commercial subjects, with every provision for research departments and administrative offices, and with the most advanced requirements for mental and physical development, this school is tremendously significant of the new South.

But perhaps the most compelling, and certainly the most picturesque of all of Winchester's signs of progressiveness is its apple industry. For these orchards that unfurl one fragrant acre of blossoms after another fill the second largest apple warehouse in the world. George Washington was much interested in pomology and we have a record of a deed given by him in 1776 requiring the purchasers to set out one hundred winter apple trees and one hundred peach trees. This orchard was the largest in the Valley at this time. Some of the trees planted by Hessian prisoners have lived for a century.

The first commercial orchard was begun about fifty years ago, by John Lupton. Although it was regarded with skepticism by the neighboring farmers, when it grew to 4000 acres and began to bring in $150,000 to $300,000 a year, they reconstructed their ideas. Now Winchester has almost four hundred orchards and harvests over a million barrels of apples yearly, and has developed the by-products into large factories for canning and evaporating, and for the making of jelly and cider and vinegar. There is a vigorous European export trade. Governor Byrd, who was a good farmer be-

THE WINCHESTER ORCHARD COUNTRY

fore he was a good governor, regularly sends half of his superfine crop to Bristol, England. All these commercial orchards are equipped with modern machinery. The Winchester Field Laboratory furnishes the fruit-growers with direct and free information on the control of fungus diseases and insect pests, while plant pathologists and entomologists continue research on these and allied subjects.

The cycle of the apple year is full of color and fragrance. First the whole Valley ripples into clouds of white, culminating with the annual apple-blossom festival of two days, a spectacle which, with its thousands of participants, floats, bands, and parades, brings visitors from all over the United States. After the brief perfumed excitement of this great celebration, the Valley settles down under the warm summer sunshine to feel the trees growing heavy with fruit: swelling, maturing, reddening, and sweetening every breeze that passes. With autumn, brightly painted carts, blue and red and yellow, loaded with fruit and drawn by two or even three teams of horses, go clattering down the streets. The brass on the harness gleams: bells tinkle and bright tassels swing. The whole city is brave and flashing with rich and pungent prosperity. Half a million dollars of new money is distributed to local labor during six to ten weeks. There has never been a labor strike here, where there are less than two per cent foreign-born.

All around Winchester are the large secluded estates so dear to the hearts and so essential to the happiness of Virginians. The seventy-five miles to Washington is a scattering succession of villages, stone walls, negro settlements with crooked walls and crazy eaves dazzling with whitewash; hedges, little stone churches, spacious manor houses set behind their lawns and box gardens; good inns where the horse-loving folk from Berryville, Warrenton, and Middleburg gather for hunt breakfasts and belated teas.

About eleven miles from Winchester and four miles off the main road stands White Post — still bearing the name that was given it when Lord Fairfax erected a white post and wrote on it the directions to Greenway Court. For it was here, in his velvet suits and waistcoats of gold tissue and scarlet plush breeches, that the misogynist lived. After the woman he had been engaged to in his youth had jilted him, and his mother and his grandmother had inveigled him out of the Fairfax estates in England, he decided he had had enough of the weaker sex and left England forever. He first took care to secure a definition of his five million acres of property in the New World on the basis of aristocratic privilege. He reserved a mere ten thousand acres for his own uses at Greenway Court, and managed to make a fortune out of the quitrents he exacted from the settlers on the rest of it. He liked to style these settlers his 'retainers,' which did not add to his popularity with them. Greenway Court, whose site may still be seen, stood for over a century, and was the center of much hospitality to men — no women ever being permitted to enter it. Lord Fairfax was public-spirited according to his lights. He advanced money to his 'retainers' for the improvement of their holdings, gave his excess revenues to the poor, and was actively patriotic during the French and Indian wars. He was one of the picturesque figures of his day, and in spite of his broken heart he lived to be ninety-one, and seems to have had a pretty good time of it. His body is buried at Winchester, his name survives in a score of places, and the impress of his vigorous personality has become a part of Virginia.

The highway from Winchester to Washington might be regarded as symbol of the old and the new. For it is most agreeably modern with its macadam

surface, its excellent grading and maintenance.
And yet on every side are century-old houses,
standing in neglected decrepitude or in remodeled
vigor by the side of river or on top of rolling hill.
At one place the road fords a stream, and our machine whirls through the water at the same moment that two pickaninnies on a single nag pick
their way across.

Virginia is old. Old customs, old houses with
many verandas still survive, because they were en-
gendered by the same hospitable climate which
sustains them to-day. The new blood pulsing
through her arteries cannot destroy her essential,
her ineradicable charm.

It is true that the beautiful State has changed
from an aristocratic to a democratic commonwealth. But it has not changed in its soft air, in the
ineffable blue of its mountains, and the winning
quality of its people. Her old claim to distinction,
based upon connection with English nobility, has
been overworked. Virginia itself confers an acco-
lade more enduring, more endearing than that bestowed by any king. Although she has lost some of
her semi-feudal characteristics that have been part
of the stock-in-trade of melodramatic historians,
she need have no fears. She perpetually creates an

atmosphere infinitely more delightful than any that could be trumped up by sentimentalists. There is no need to hark back to the glories that have departed, for glory is still here. There is no need even to resent the rich and hopeful Northerner who comes down to buy an old estate, fancying that thereby he may become a Southern gentleman.

So miraculous is this leisurely sunshine, so subtle is the sense of happiness that filters through the air, that it works perpetual transformations. Perhaps he may become one, after all!

THE END

Date Due

	PRINTED	IN U. S. A.	

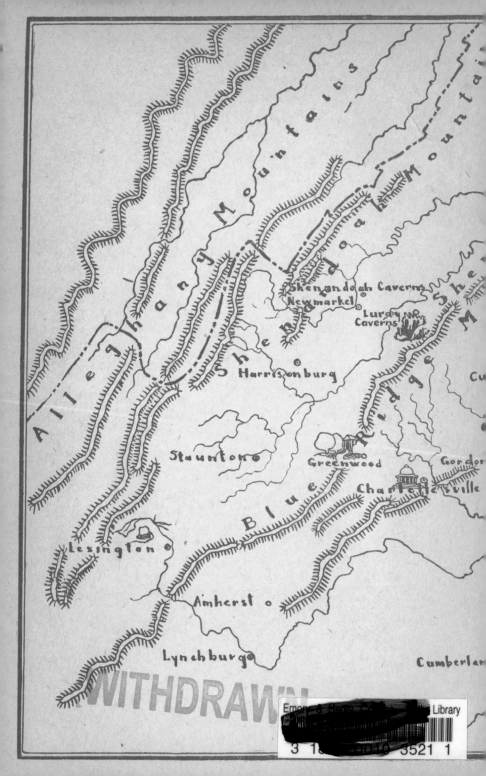